Reading Power

Revised and Expanded

Adrienne Gear

Stenhouse Publishers
PORTLAND, MAINE

Pembroke Publishers Limited
MARKHAM, ONTARIO

DEDICATION

With a full heart and the deepest of gratitude I dedicate this book to the memory of my mum and dad, Irv and Sheila Gear.

© 2015 Pembroke Publishers
538 Hood Road
Markham, Ontario, Canada L3R 3K9
www.pembrokepublishers.com

Published in the U.S. by Stenhouse Publishers
480 Congress Street
Portland, ME 04101
www.stenhouse.com

Library and Archives Canada Cataloguing in Publication

Gear, Adrienne, author
    Reading power : teaching students to think while they read / Adrienne Gear. --
Revised and expanded.

Includes bibliographical references and index.
Issued also in electronic format.
ISBN 978-1-55138-310-1 (paperback).--ISBN 978-1-55138-913-4 (pdf)

    1. Reading comprehension. 2. Reading (Elementary). I. Title.

LB1525.7.G42 2015   372.47   C2015-903653-4
                                           C2015-903654-2

Editor: Kat Mototsune
Cover Design: John Zehethofer
Typesetting: Jay Tee Graphics Ltd.

Printed and bound in Canada
9 8 7 6 5 4 3 2 1

FSC
www.fsc.org
MIX
Paper from
responsible sources
FSC® C004071

Contents

Preface to the 2nd Edition *5*
Acknowledgments *6*

Introduction *9*

Comprehension Research *9*
How Reading Power Began *11*

1 What Is Reading Power? *13*

Reading, Thinking, and Teaching *13*
Current Reading Practice *15*
Balanced Literacy Instruction *16*
Key Concepts of Reading Power *17*
    Metacognition *17*
    Interacting with Text *19*
    Developing a Common Language of Thinking *21*
    Levels of Understanding Text *21*
Teaching the Reading Powers *22*
Using Reading Power *22*
Myths about Reading Power *23*

2 The Components of Reading Power *27*

The Reading Powers Model *27*
    Helping Students Become Metacognitive *27*
    What Does Thinking Look Like? *27*
    Introducing the Thinking Brain *29*
The Reading Power Theme Song *32*
Reading Power Book Collections *32*
    Reading Power Books *34*
    Creating a Reading Power Book Collection *35*
Reading Power Instruction *37*
    Modeling *37*
    Components of Reading Power Instruction *40*

3 The Power to Connect *43*

New Thinking About Connecting *45*
    Going Deeper with Connections *45*
    Brain Pockets *45*
Sequential Lessons for Connecting *46*

Assessing Connections *54*
Connect Books *55*

4 The Power to Visualize *67*

New Thinking about Visualizing *68*
Sequential Lessons for Visualizing *69*
Assessing Visualizing *77*
Visualize Books *77*

5 The Power to Question *89*

New Thinking about Questioning *91*
 Questions that Matter *91*
 Quick and Deep-Thinking Questions *91*
Sequential Lessons for Questioning *92*
Assessing Questions *99*
Question Books *99*

6 The Power to Infer *108*

New Thinking about Inferring *111*
Sequential Lessons for Inferring *111*
Assessing Inferencing *118*
Infer Books *118*

7 The Power to Transform *128*

New Thinking about Transform *132*
Sequential Lessons for Transform *132*
Assessing Transformed Thinking *139*
Transform Books *140*

8 Application and Assessment *150*

Students Using the Reading Powers *150*
Reading Power and Literature Circles *154*
 Before You Start *155*
 Getting Started *156*
 Additional Response Activities *156*
 Lit Circle Assessment *157*
 Recommended Books for Lit Circles *157*
Reading Power and Parents *170*
Assessment *172*
 Goals of Reading Comprehension *172*

Final Thoughts *185*
Heads-Up Teaching *186*

Professional Resources *187*

Index *189*

Preface to the 2nd Edition

Reading Power is a practical approach to comprehension instruction developed ten years ago at my school in Vancouver, B.C. Currently, it is being implemented in many schools in British Columbia and across Canada, and in parts of the US, the UK, and Australia. It is a way of teaching reading comprehension that focuses readers' attention on their thinking as they read, using authentic children's literature to support the lessons.

Reading Power was launched at Laura Secord Elementary School in Vancouver in October 2002. Initially it was developed for primary teachers at that school as an initiative towards their involvement in the Vancouver School Board's Early Literacy Project. Since then, Reading Power has been enthusiastically embraced by teachers, support teachers, teacher-librarians, and administrators, all of whom share a common goal: to help their students become better readers. For more than a decade, I have witnessed Reading Power evolving in my own classroom and many others. I have watched and listened as students learn to think through texts rather than simply decoding them. I have gained valuable insight and understanding into what it means to be an active, engaged reader and thinker. Through my own teaching, workshops, and conversations with teachers, I have continued to revisit the big ideas and key concepts of Reading Power and have learned a great deal.

I have heard expressed during literacy conferences and symposiums that the greatest contribution to a child's literacy progress is exemplary teaching practices. I can say, without a doubt, that there is not one teacher I have worked with since Reading Power was published who does not demonstrate exemplary teaching. It is the dedication to learning of all who have attended my workshops, read my books, or tried some of these lessons to which I owe great admiration and gratitude. You have provided me with the valuable insights, important questions, and amazing adaptations of lessons that has made Reading Power what it is today.

Reading Power was first published in 2006. It is hard to believe that nearly 10 years has passed since its release. From its humble beginnings, as scribbles on a napkin at my friend's kitchen table, it has changed and grown. It is a fascinating process to read (and reread!) my original thoughts and ideas about Reading Power when it was in its beginning stages. After so many years of teaching and talking about comprehension instruction with students and teachers, much of my thinking has evolved. Some of the things I deemed important then are not as important now, while others now seem essential. The basic fundamentals remain; however, a great deal of new thinking and understanding about purpose and pedagogy has emerged. As I like to tell teachers in my workshops, best practice evolves from reflecting and refining. And that is just what I hope this new edition of *Reading Power* is going to accomplish—reflecting and refining my thinking about comprehension instruction and what we, as teachers, can continue to do to help our students develop as thinkers of text, as well as decoders of text. Yes, it is still all about thinking. But it's also about how we get our students to notice, reflect, and refine their thinking so that reading becomes a more interactive and meaningful experience. I am excited to share how Reading Power has evolved over the years through new lessons, new templates, and, of course, new book lists (my favorite part!). For those of you already familiar with Reading Power, I invite you to read this book through the lens of your experiences with teaching the strategies, revisiting these ideas with me. For those new to Reading Power, I hope this book nudges your thinking and provides for you a new way of looking at comprehension and instruction.

Some of the changes in this edition include a section of new thinking about each of the reading powers with an emphasis on how to help students go deeper with their thinking. New templates and assessment rubrics are also included, as well as a more comprehensive section on Literature Circles and how to encourage parents to use Reading Power strategies at home. Because Reading Power is now being used in some middle and high schools, my book lists have been extended to include recommendations for older students, as well as some sidebar tips for using Reading Power in the upper grades. I have also discovered important links between some of the strategies: Connecting and Visualizing are closely linked by a reader's memories and experiences; Questioning and Inferring are closely linked by the scaffolding of thinking. I therefore recommend a revised order for teaching the strategies to reflect these links: Connect, Visualize, Question, Infer, and Transform.

Acknowledgments

The expression "It takes a village…" describes my sentiments when considering the number of people who, directly or indirectly, have been involved in *Reading Power*. This work is a reflection of many dedicated classroom teachers, support teachers, teacher-librarians, administrators, consultants, colleagues, friends, and family who have been supporting my efforts for many years.

Reading Power began at Laura Secord Elementary School in Vancouver. It was there I developed the idea, and I will always be grateful to the staff and students I worked with during those early stages. They helped me turn my vision into something that could be implemented into classrooms, gave me valuable insights and suggestions, and allowed me into their classrooms to try out lessons.

I also am indebted to the staff and students at my current school, J.W. Sexsmith Elementary. As Reading Power evolved, I was able to work with this amazing group of educators, teaching and learning along with them. In particular, I want to acknowledge the students I have had the privilege of teaching over the years. Their enthusiasm for Reading Power and their willingness to rise to the challenge of thinking about reading in a new way has made this journey enormously worthwhile. They have taught me more than I could ever teach them.

I continue to be inspired by the hundreds of teachers, teacher-librarians, and administrators with whom I have worked across the province and country over the past years. It is a privilege to be in a position where I am in contact with many dedicated educators in pursuit of enhancing their reading programs, not by a "quick fix" but through a deeper understanding of reading and thinking. These teachers have worked hard to support the implementation of Reading Power in their schools by organizing workshops, book bins, and demo lessons, and by providing time for teachers to meet, reflect, and share ideas around best practices in reading instruction.

A special thank-you to Kyla Hadden, extraordinary secondary teacher in SD 83 (North-Okanagan Shuswap). Many secondary teachers believed that Reading Power was for elementary students, but Kyla knew from the early days that Reading Power is not limited to certain grades, but is instead grounded in the principals of metacognition and best practice. Passionate about children's literature and already using picture books with her senior-high students, she thought outside the box and successfully adapted Reading Power lessons for older grades. I am grateful for her inspiration and for spreading the Reading Power "word" to her students and colleagues. She contributed many of the tips and book recommendations for older students for this edition.

There are many people who have, over the years, inspired me to evolve into not only a teacher of students but also a teacher of teachers. I am grateful to Ruth Wrinch, former Vancouver administrator, who was my first mentor. She taught me, through example, the art of listening and was instrumental in my pursuit of knowledge, change, and best classroom practices.

I'd like to acknowledge some important people in my life and work who, over the years, have made me a better teacher, person, and friend; Cheryl Burian, Kimberly Matterson, Donna Boardman, Katie McCormack, Sue Stevenson, Jen Daerendinger, Kathy Keeler, Kimberley Stacey, Stephanie Yorath, Carrie Gelson, and Amy Wou. Special thanks to Lisa Wilson and Donna Kosak, my literacy soul sisters from SD 23 and enthusiastic recipients of my "valet lessons"!

Special thanks to my dearest friend, Cheryl Burian, for her support and for Reading Power as it evolved from its earliest stages on a napkin in her kitchen until now. Thank you for inspiring me to pursue my passion, regardless of the disappointments and challenges I faced along the way. You have always expected nothing less than the best from me, yet shown me nothing but love while I try to achieve it. I couldn't ask for a better friend.

Thank you to my friend and fellow Vancouver teacher Carrie Gelson, who not only is a brilliant teacher, a passionate child advocate, and an amazing blogger, but also loves books as much as I do! I am grateful to her for opening up the world of social media to me and inspiring me to blog and Tweet about the books I love.

Always much love and thanks to my book club. I look forward to our monthly meetings, where I am surrounded by my favorite things—good friends and good books! (Okay, the wine is usually pretty good too!) Thank you Cheryl, Krista, Anna, Laura G., Laura B., Stella, Melanie, Heather, Bonnie, Jarma, and Maria.

I am indebted to Mary Macchiusi, my publisher and friend, and the amazing family at Pembroke. Ten years and five books later, I could not be in better hands. Enormous gratitude to my brilliant editor, Kat Mototsune, who has patiently guided me, with precision and clarity, to make this edition immeasurably better.

Continued gratitude and acknowledgment to the incredible staff at Vancouver Kidsbooks, particularly co-owner Phyllis Simon and store managers Leslie Buffman (Kitsilano), Susan McGuigan (Edgemont), and Maggie Blondeau (Surrey, recently closed) for providing teachers and teacher-librarians an invaluable source of outstanding children's literature to support their literacy programs. The staff have been instrumental in helping teachers from all over the province begin to create their Reading Power book bins, and I am grateful for all their support.

I extend my enormous gratitude to the staff at United Library Services (B.C. and Alberta), particularly Elizabeth Graves, Natalie Fortune, manager Ria

Bleumer at the Burnaby Warehouse; Robin Hoogwerf, ULS General Manager, and Diane Langston, Manager of Children's Books & Schools. They have been instrumental in providing the very best books at the very best price for teachers across the western provinces, and always welcome me into their warehouse with a coffee and an empty shopping cart.

Finally, to my family: my love and enormous gratitude to my late parents, Irv and Sheila Gear, for teaching me the value of education, the blessings of stories, and to follow my passion. Thank you to my sisters Alison and Janet for their unwavering support and belief in me. I remain eternally grateful to my husband Richard Gatzke, who said to me once, "It must be very tiring living inside your head." He continues to keep me grounded in the important things and supports my numerous pursuits with quiet loyalty and love. Finally, I want to thank my two boys, Spencer and Oliver, who have, without *question*, *connected* me to the beauty and energy of the inquiring mind, and have *transformed* my *vision* of love.

Introduction

Influenced by the book *Strategies That Work: Teaching Comprehension to Enhance Understanding* by Stephanie Harvey and Anne Goudvis (2000), and by the work of many researchers in the field of reading, including P. David Pearson, Reading Power is an approach to comprehension instruction designed to teach students specific metacognitive strategies to use during the reading process that enable them to engage in a more interactive, thoughtful reading experience. Central to the Reading Power approach is authentic children's literature for modeling demonstrations, practice, and independent reading.

Comprehension Research

In the 1970s, an educator and researcher by the name of David Pearson, a professor at the University of Michigan, embarked on a study of proficient readers. In lay terms, he wanted to know what made "this child" a better reader than "this child." What was it that readers exceeding expectations for their grade level were doing that enabled them to master both the code and the meaning of the text? During this extensive study, his team of researchers studied the profile of dozens of proficient readers. After several years and a careful analysis of an enormous amount of data, Pearson determined several common strategies used by proficient readers that enabled them to make sense of what they were reading. A condensed version of this research is what I describe as the "profile" of a proficient reader.

Profile of a Proficient Reader

A proficient, engaged reader is **metacognitive**—aware of and able to use and articulate the following strategies in order to interact with the text:

1. Make Connections. A good reader is able to draw from background knowledge and personal experiences while reading to help create meaning from the text.

2. Ask Questions. A good reader asks both literal and inferential questions before, during, and after reading to clarify and deepen understanding.

3. Visualize. A good reader is able to create multi-sensory images in the "mind's eye" while reading to help make sense of the text.

4. Draw Inferences. A good reader knows that not all information is included in a text, and is able to draw conclusions from both picture and word clues, combined with his or her own knowledge to "fill in" what is not directly written.

5. Determine Importance. A good reader sifts through information in the text to select key ideas and to summarize and remember them.

6. Analyze and Synthesize. A good reader is able to break down information and to draw conclusions and acquire new thinking based on both the text and his or her own thinking.

7. Monitor Comprehension. A good reader is aware when understanding is being compromised and is able to stop, go back, and reread in order for understanding to occur.

More than thirty years later, David Pearson's research has found its way into teacher education, professional development, and classroom practice. The common strategies used by proficient readers are now being taught to readers of all grades and all levels of reading. They are integrated into Canadian curricula and are an important component in the Common Core Reading Standards in the US. Simply stated, if these strategies are what research has found that good readers do to understand text, then these are the strategies we need to be teaching to all of our students. Over 20 years of research and experience, there has been a dramatic shift in our understanding and approach to reading comprehension.

WHAT IS READING COMPREHENSION

Before	After
• "Read the passage, then answer the comprehension questions."	• Interaction with a text.
• Most questions are literal.	• Book + Thinking = Understanding.
• Answers are found in the text.	• A focus on constructing meaning
• Answers are right or wrong.	• "Reading happens in two places: in the book and in your brain."
• Lack of instruction from teacher: *assign and assess*.	• Metacognition
	• Explicit instruction and teacher modeling
	• Developing a common language of thinking.

I had the pleasure of hearing David Pearson speak at a conference in Vancouver several years ago. I sat in the front row, clapping very loudly. (During his presentation, I wished I had a lighter with me—as at a rock concert—to shine and wave in support of his wise words.) He spoke of his research, and of implementing change in the way we need to think about reading and to teach students to read. Reading, he stated, is not simply mastering the code. Reading is both the code and meaning behind that code. And while many teachers make the assumption that once the code is mastered, so too is comprehension, we now realize that if we want our students to acquire the ability to comprehend texts, we need to balance our reading instruction to include explicit teaching both in decoding and in comprehension. The work of Stephanie Harvey and Anne Goudvis, much of which is based on David Pearson's research, reflects the complexity of comprehension and its nature as a separate, yet equally important, aspect of reading. They state, "Reading demands a two-pronged attack. It involves cracking the alphabetic code to determine the words and thinking about those words to construct meaning." (2000, p. 5)

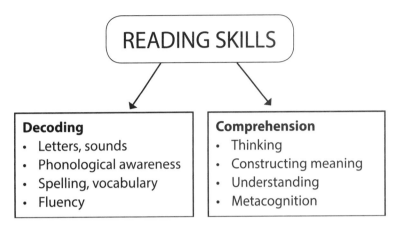

This graphic helps illustrate the point made by Harvey and Goudvis. The skills listed on the left are those essential to mastering the code, and are generally taught in the early primary grades. They are the basics of beginning reading instruction—taught in a variety of different approaches and methods, but certainly the main focus in early primary Language Arts programs. Often the assumption is made that, once students have mastered the code, comprehension (made up of the skills listed on the right) occurs naturally. But while this is true for some students, it is not the case for most. David Pearson's research points to comprehension as a separate aspect of reading, one that requires the same amount of direct instruction and teaching time as the decoding skills. "Once thought of as a natural result of decoding plus oral language, comprehension is now viewed as a much more complex process involving knowledge, experience, thinking and teaching." (Fielding and Pearson, pp. 62–67)

In other words, if we are to help improve our students' ability to comprehend text and learn to actively construct meaning for themselves, we need to devote as much direct instructional time teaching *thinking* as we do teaching *decoding*. When we consider the number of instructional minutes primary teachers spend on teaching code, that means significant changes to some reading programs. Reading instruction can no longer be considered the responsibility of early primary teachers; it is the responsibility of all teachers. All teachers need to consider themselves teachers of reading, and reading instruction must continue throughout all elementary and high-school grades. If mastering the code is only one aspect of learning to read, then teaching the code is only one aspect of reading instruction. Children need to learn that reading is not simply words on a page, but what those words mean to them. Teaching them how to make sense of those words is just as important as teaching them how to read them.

How Reading Power Began

In 2001, the school where I was teaching in Vancouver, Laura Secord Elementary, we began to notice a something interesting when analyzing reading assessments: scores for decoding and running records were much higher than comprehension scores. Students were clearly "reading," but not necessarily understanding what they were reading. As a staff, we set a school goal to focus on and try to improve

"There are literally hundreds of strategies we can choose to teach our students how to become better readers. The key is, everyone on your staff chooses the same ones and uses the same language to talk about them."
—David Pearson, from a speech at Vancouver Technical Secondary, Vancouver, Fall 2003

I can still remember one staff member, after my initial presentation of Reading Power to my staff, stating that his plate was already full and that he "didn't have time to teach thinking"!

comprehension scores and somehow try to bridge this gap. We had spent the previous years focusing on phonemic awareness, but it was becoming apparent that many of our students were not understanding much of what they were now able to decode. It was during those early meetings and discussions on the literacy goals of our school that my thoughts turned to Stephanie Harvey and Anne Goudvis' book, *Strategies That Work*. I reviewed the book and pulled out things that I thought could be implemented easily, adding my own ideas and my passion for children's literature. Reading Power was born.

Clarity and simplicity were my priorities when developing Reading Power. I knew how hard teachers work and how many demands are placed on us each year, so I knew that adding one more thing to the teaching plate was not going to be something everyone would welcome. I also knew that we, as a staff, had already been implementing many strategies from many different sources.

If I handed out the Profile of a Proficient Reader (page 9) to my colleagues and said, "These are the strategies we need to be teaching our kids to help them become better readers," the reaction might not have been very positive. I knew that, in order for us to try something new in the classroom, it needed to be simple and practical. I looked carefully over the Profile and decided that seven strategies were simply too many to realistically expect teachers to teach and apply to their reading program, so I chose five of them: connect, question, visualize, infer, and synthesize (transform). The strategies I did not choose are in no way less important. These five were chosen simply because of a belief that they were the ones I felt were most relevant to teaching fiction and that teachers could most easily implement.

When streamlining the Profile of a Proficient Reader, I changed the word from *synthesize* to *transform* because I felt it was simpler language for young children. Most children are familiar with a "transformer" toy that changes from one form to another and the movies that those toys spawned. The notion of a change in thinking seemed to be easier to describe to a young child by using the word "transform."

As a teacher, I believe routine is important for student learning. I work best when I know what I'm doing and when I'm doing it, and so do my students. In this book, I strived to develop a sequential pattern that is consistent, regardless of the Reading Power strategy you are teaching. By following it, both you and your students will find a familiar routine as you work through the reading powers. In each chapter devoted to a reading power you will find

- a strategy song
- sequential lessons, including an introduction lesson for the reading power
- a sample anchor chart
- an assessment rubric
- updated book lists
- reproducible templates for use with the lessons

Regardless of the strategies you choose—from the list of strategies that make up the Profile of a Proficient Reader, from the reading powers, or from another source—and the number you choose to introduce during the course of the school year, what is important is for everyone on your staff to make a commitment to intentionally integrate the strategies and the "language of thinking" into their daily practice. I have found that, in many schools, these same strategies are being taught, but teachers are using slightly different language to teach them. Creating a common language across the grades in a school becomes instrumental in a child's development as a reader. Common language, weaving through the fabric of the classrooms in a school, creates a quilt of understanding.

1 What Is Reading Power?

The five reading strategies in the Reading Power approach are called reading "powers," because the word "strategy" has been used to describe just about anything done in the classroom, and is often used interchangeably with the word "activity." The five reading powers are, in fact, reading strategies. Reading Power became my catchphrase for comprehension instruction. I called it Reading Power because it is more appealing to children, when they see it on their Shape of the Day, than Comprehension Instruction.

Reading Power
- is based on research that looks at strategies used by proficient readers.
- teaches students that reading is thinking.
- teaches students to be metacognitive, or aware of their thinking.
- creates a "common language of thinking" in your classroom and school.
- teaches students five strategies to enhance their understanding of the fiction texts they are reading: the powers to Connect, Visualize, Question, Infer, and Transform.
- encourages students to have "busy brains" while they read.
- provides a concrete visual tool to help teach the five reading powers.
- exposes students to a wide range of rich, engaging literature—including both old classics and wonderful new titles.
- can be used to enhance your writing program.
- is respectful of children's thinking and encourages them to think beyond the pages of the books they are reading.
- celebrates the students' voices in the classroom and allows for their thinking, their connections, their images, and their ideas to make a difference.
- results in rich, engaging, and interactive lessons in which students are encouraged to share their thinking.
- will change the way you and your students read and think.

Reading, Thinking, and Teaching

A mother and son, who is not yet school age, sit facing each other on the floor in the living room, each reading a book. Their "noisy reading" time, when Mom reads aloud to her child, is over, and now they are sharing in their "quiet reading" ritual. Mom senses her son is not engaged on this particular day, and notices that he keeps looking up from his book to stare at her. After a while, she asks him what he is doing.

"I'm watching to see what happens."

"What happens in my book?" she asks.

"No… what happens when you read."

"Oh," she answers, and goes back to reading.

The boy continues to watch his mother intently while she reads. "Mom," the boy asks finally, "what really happens to you when you read?"

This young boy has, in his simplicity, asked a most profound question. The notion of "something happening" while we read is the essence of comprehension. The "something happening" is the interactive construction of meaning inside our heads, which creates understanding. Because thinking is an abstract concept, the "something happening" can be difficult to see, difficult to understand, difficult to assess, and difficult to teach. And sadly, the "something happening" does not naturally occur inside all readers.

Because reading comprehension is not tangible and can be subjective, it is a subject that many teachers do not necessarily delve into the first week in their school year. Certainly it was not, up until a few years ago, a subject that found a spot on my weekly timetable or a place in my "shape of the day." In fact, there was no time in my school year that I could honestly say was devoted to direct comprehension instruction. Why? If I look back on my own education, I do not recall any reading instruction other than the decoding and phonemic awareness I received in the early primary grades. In university, I do not recall any methodology courses on comprehension instruction.

I began my teaching career as an intermediate teacher. As a new intermediate teacher, I considered my job to be somehow more interesting than that of my primary teacher colleagues. Thanks to the hard work of those primary teachers, my students could, for the most part, already read when they came into my class in September. I'm embarrassed to admit that I clearly remember saying to a friend that the reason I enjoyed teaching intermediate grades so much was that I didn't have to teach reading and could do "fun stuff" with the students. I truly believed the expression, "Learn to read in the primary grades and read to learn in the intermediate grades." I never considered myself a teacher of reading. We did reading in my class, but it was not something that I taught. I did not need to teach reading—my students already knew how.

I now realize that my rendition of "doing reading" was "Read this chapter and then answer these questions"—what is now termed *assign-and-assess* teaching. And when a student was able to answer only two out of the ten questions correctly, what was I doing to help? Usually I handed back the notebook with the message, "*Please do your corrections,*" along with a sparkly sticker stating, "Good effort!" or "Nice printing!" The thought of it now makes me cringe—how little I was doing to help my students become better readers. Sure, my students were read to every day; my classroom was overflowing with literature; we did novel studies, book reports, story maps, letters to the authors, book talks; we wrote reading response logs, made dioramas, created posters, did readers theatre, and did all the "fun stuff" I believed fell under the category of teaching reading.

Looking back, I wonder how many of those activities represented a deep understanding of text. Certainly my students enjoyed the process and were proud of their products. But I realize now that I was not, under any circumstances, teaching them how to use their experiences and their knowledge to make sense of what they were reading. I was at the helm of a sinking ship, handing out brushes and paint to my students and teaching them how to paint the decks. Showing children that reading is not just words on a page, helping them see what of ourselves we bring to those words, is perhaps the single most important thing we can do, not only to keep our ships afloat, but also to send them full-speed ahead.

Current Reading Practice

When reflecting on my earlier years of teaching, I recall dedicated teachers who were all working towards enhancing their classroom practice in the area of literacy. Many, including myself, had attended after-school workshops and professional development on current literacy practices, and had already begun implementing many of these strategies. When trying to implement change, I believe it is important to begin to look at the things one is already doing well, so I remember a meeting where my colleagues and I discussed and brainstormed all the literacy initiatives, strategies, and activities we were currently practicing in our classrooms. The list was long and represented a wealth of rich and engaging classroom practices. After analyzing this list carefully, I found it interesting to see exactly where our reading instruction occurred in the reading process.

Three Stages of Teaching Reading

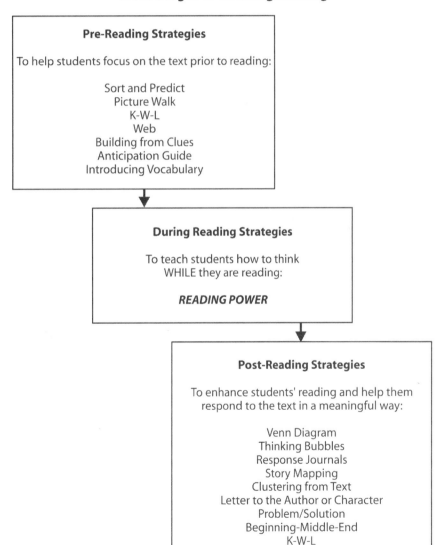

Pre-Reading Strategies

To help students focus on the text prior to reading:

Sort and Predict
Picture Walk
K-W-L
Web
Building from Clues
Anticipation Guide
Introducing Vocabulary

During Reading Strategies

To teach students how to think
WHILE they are reading:

READING POWER

Post-Reading Strategies

To enhance students' reading and help them
respond to the text in a meaningful way:

Venn Diagram
Thinking Bubbles
Response Journals
Story Mapping
Clustering from Text
Letter to the Author or Character
Problem/Solution
Beginning-Middle-End
K-W-L

If we look at the reading process as three equally important stages—pre-reading, during-reading, and post-reading—everything we were doing in our reading program fell in either the pre-reading and post-reading stages (see The Three Stages of Teaching Reading chart on page 15). Prior to reading, we spent time building up interest in the text with predictions, picture walks, and K–W–L. Then either the students would read independently or we would read to them. After reading, the students would be engaged in various post-reading activities.

There was a big gap in the during-reading stage of my teaching. What were we teaching our students to do when the book was in their hands and their eyes were on the words? And since, according to Pearson's research, comprehension occurs while we are *in the act of reading*, those during-reading strategies hold the key to understanding. I realized that teaching children specific strategies for the during-reading process was the piece that had been missing from my reading program, and the hole left by that missing piece kept getting bigger each year. As a teacher, I consider myself first and foremost a learner. Having not only learned what was missing in my practice, but also trying to find a way to fill in the missing piece, I was learning the most valuable lesson of my teaching journey.

Balanced Literacy Instruction

My goal is that my students leave my classroom in June better readers than they were when they arrived in September. How this happens is through direct, ongoing, explicit instruction and providing students with time to read independently and practice what they learn. As their teacher, it is my responsibility to ensure that this happens.

As a "seasoned" teacher, one of the things I have learned is the value of reflecting and refining. Reflecting on practice has made me a better teacher because I am always searching for ways to make my teaching better for my students. And while it is both a blessing and a curse to be in a constant state of reflection, Reading Power would never have been developed had I not reflected on what wasn't working in my reading program.

When beginning a workshop, I often ask teachers to reflect on their reading program, asking them to divide a circle into pieces. On each piece they are to record one element of their reading program, including all experiences in which their students are engaged in reading; for example, silent reading, buddy reading, read-aloud, literature circles, morning message, phonics, readers theatre, etc. I then ask them to put a star in the pieces where they are providing direct, explicit instruction in some aspect of reading.

SLICES OF THE READING PROGRAM

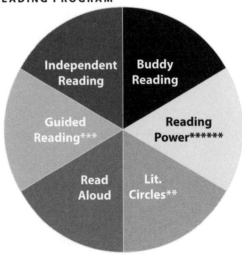

The Balanced Literacy Diet is a web site with video clips of effective literacy-enriched classrooms. Look for the clip of a teacher explaining how she incorporates Reading Power with the Daily 5 and CAFE.

Over several years of teaching Reading Power, I have noticed that the language of thinking that students learn during those lessons become integrated into other aspects of my reading program. Moreover, it also has spilled over into content areas, such as Math, Science, and Social Studies. We will often *make connections* in Socials, *visualize* while trying to solve a Math problem, and *infer* during a Science experiment.

Ten years ago, my Reading Program graph would have included a lot of "doing" reading activities, with very little explicit instruction in reading skills and strategies. Now, the addition of Reading Power, or comprehension instruction, makes comprehension instruction an essential piece of my reading program. The only way our students are going to develop as readers and thinkers is if we teach them. I can't imagine, in fact, having a reading program that does not include some kind of ongoing, explicit instruction in thinking.

I would recommend blocking off two periods of approximately 40 minutes each per week to focus on Reading Power lessons. This allows time for you to incorporate other components of your literacy program, such as guided reading, Daily 5, literature circles, and buddy reading. The strategies and the language of thinking that students learn in those two blocks of Reading Power can be applied to the other components. Reading Power, in fact, ties in effectively with the Daily 5 and CAFE components of a literacy program. For example, students can work on specific strategies they learn through Reading Power lessons during "read to self" or "read to someone" choices from the Daily 5. I view Reading Power as the essential foundation on which all other aspects of my literacy program lie.

The purpose of the Slices of the Reading Program exercise is to encourage teachers to reflect on their practice and to notice how much or how little time they are spending on direct, explicit reading instruction. While we might think we have a full and enriched reading program, with many hours a week in which are students are engaged in reading activities, it is important to ask ourselves how many of those experiences would be considered "doing reading" compared to "teaching reading." While some consider reading instruction to be the primary responsibility of early primary teachers, I believe explicit instruction in reading is the responsibility of every teacher, no matter what grade they teach. If students already know how to decode, then we need to provide them with instruction in the other part of reading—the thinking part.

Key Concepts of Reading Power

Metacognition

Years before I had developed Reading Power, I had an experience in my classroom that was instrumental to my teaching and learning. I was teaching a Grade 5 class and, during silent reading, would call students up to my desk individually to conference with me. I made notes about their miscues, reading strategies, and fluency, and then usually asked them a few questions about the text. One day, it was Simon's turn to come to my desk. Simon was an ESL learner, having immigrated to Canada with his family from Guatemala when he was three. He was a lively, personable child who communicated well. He happily came to my desk, sat beside me, and began reading aloud from his chapter book. He read with fluency and expression, and demonstrated many of the decoding strategies he had learned in his previous grades. I was impressed with his reading and told him so. Had I stopped there, I would have made some huge assumptions of what kind of reader he was. But then I began asking him a few questions from the story. Simon was not able to answer a single question. I remember feeling completely shocked at his lack of understanding, and wondered how it could be possible for a student to be reading the words from a text so well, yet not have a single idea about what he was reading. I remember turning to Simon and asking him,

"Aren't you thinking about the story when you read it?" After a moment's pause, Simon turned to me and asked, "What does thinking look like?" It was probably the most important question anyone has ever asked me. At the time, I could not really answer him: "Thinking is… well… it's just thinking!" was certainly not the answer he was looking for. Now I wish that I could find Simon and tell him that I can finally answer his question.

Simon's profound question has stayed with me over the years. I think many teachers have had similar experiences with their own Simons—children who become so focused on the code that they forget to really think about the story. Simon showed me a missing piece to the reading puzzle. I was doing so much with my students in terms of reading, yet the part I was *not* doing seemed to be the most important—"Whoops! Sorry, kids, I almost forgot to tell you this tidbit of information: when you read, you also need to think"! What I did not realize then, but do now, was that this experience informed my understanding of what I now believe is the most important component of helping children become more proficient readers: metacognition.

"Metacognition" was a new buzz word when I was doing courses for my Masters degree at the University of British Columbia nearly 15 years ago. Although I did not fully understand it then, I certainly made the effort to insert it into my papers as often as I could, so I could present myself to my learned professors as being in touch with the current lingo. Now, many years and experiences later, the concept of *metacognition* or "thinking about your thinking" has become an important component of the Language Arts curriculum and an equally important component in my teaching practice. Over the years, I realize that it is more than just "thinking about your thinking" that is important. Being able to talk about your thinking is also an essential part of being metacognitive. I now see metacognition now as having three essential components: awareness of your thinking; thinking about your thinking; and articulating your thinking.

And so it became important to me, when developing Reading Power, to let students in on the secret: The secret to becoming a successful reader is to learn to think while you read. And I wanted to show children the answer to Simon's question: *What does thinking look like?* I wanted to provide children with something concrete and visual so that they could really see what a thinking brain looks like when it's reading. It was essential that this metacognition be somehow incorporated into Reading Power as a concrete image that could be a point of reference. Simply put, if Simon's head was empty, I needed to fill it up with five reading powers. And that was how the Reading Powers Model (see page 28) was born. I roughly drew it on a napkin and presented it to my staff, then drew and colored a poster of the model for every primary classroom in my school. The common language of reading comprehension naturally emerged from the use of the Reading Powers Model, and the Reading Power slogan became "Fill Your Head with Reading Power."

It is important to mention that, after teaching Reading Power to hundreds of children, it has become clear to me that children's brains are not empty at all. In fact, their brains are already filled with these strategies. The only problem is that students aren't necessarily aware of them. Our job, as teachers, is not to fill their brains, but to focus their brains on the cognitive strategies that are already in their heads, and to provide them with the language to describe them.

"Reading furnishes the mind only with materials of knowledge; it is thinking that makes what we read ours."
—John Locke

Active Readers…	We Can Help By…
• use specific strategies while they read to help make sense of the text.	• providing students with a common language of strategies used by proficient readers.
• are metacognitive, or aware that their thinking plays an important role in their understanding of the text.	• introduce students to metacognition— an awareness of thinking.
• pay attention to their "thinking voice" while they read to help them make sense of the text.	• model think-alouds so that the students can begin to see what thinking looks and sounds like.

Interacting with Text

Another key concept of Reading Power is the idea of interacting with text. Interacting—that is, the equal sharing between text and reader—is important to explain to students.

I usually begin the lesson by drawing two people on the board who are engaged in a conversation. Speaking bubbles are added to the picture, as well as a double-sided arrow between the figures.

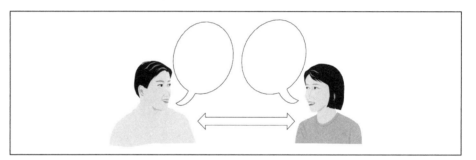

Today we are going to learn an important word that is going to help us understand what good readers need to do.

(Draw figure on the board)

Invite the students to discuss the picture and ask them to think of some other words that could describe what is going on in the picture.

(talking, conversing, sharing, back-and-forth)

Explain that the important thing to remember about interacting is that it is equal.

These two people are both talking and being given equal opportunities to contribute to the conversation. This makes for an interesting and engaging conversation.

Draw the next example on the board and ask the students to discuss what is happening.

One-Sided Conversation

Explain that, in this picture, only one person is being given a chance to contribute to the conversation. Explain that sometimes only one person is speaking, such as in a classroom or a workshop, but that if you are talking to a friend and they don't give you a chance to speak, often you lose interest and become bored.

Now draw a picture of a person but tell the students that you are going to replace the other person with a book to show a reader who is interacting with a text. Invite students to talk about what they think that means.

Interacting with Text

Interaction means a give and take. When people interact with a text, they take in the story or information from the book, but also give back their thinking. Interacting with a book means that a reader adds their thinking into the story by connecting, questioning, visualizing, inferring, and transforming while they read. If we don't add our own thinking into a story, we will more likely start to lose interest and become bored. Having a one-sided conversation with a book is not going to help us understand the book at all.

Finally, present a graphic that shows what reading and thinking look like.

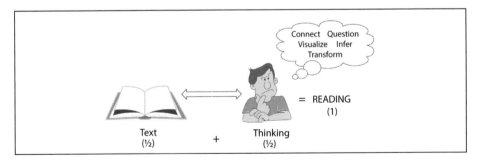

Interacting with Text Equation

Developing a Common Language of Thinking

When I heard David Pearson speak at a conference a number of years ago, he reflected that many of the children he observed reading for his research study were using comprehension strategies but were not able to articulate their thinking because they did not have the language to talk about it. He spoke of the importance of developing a common language of thinking within a school so that children hear the same words being used from class to class, from grade to grade. While many teachers could be teaching these strategies, they might not all be using the same language to describe them. Developing a common language of thinking in your school is the most significant factor in the successful implementation of comprehension instruction and the development of metacognition. Just as we have a common language in Math, with students hearing the same words for strategies, such as *add*, *subtract*, *multiply*, and *divide*, in any classroom from any teacher, so, too, must we develop a language to use when we talk about reading and thinking. Children quickly pick up on the language we model. I recall the excitement I felt when beginning to teach Reading Power at hearing students share their connections and questions. I recall in particular a little boy in Grade 1 who was waving his hand furiously during story time and, when asked, shouted excitedly, "I'm having a connection!"

Levels of Understanding Text

One of the ways I have grown to understand my students as readers is to observe the way they engage in text and to ask myself questions about how they make sense of what they are reading. While many formal reading assessments exist to help determine this, I am not giving my students formal reading assessments every week. I do, however, want to be able to get some sense of their level of comprehension when I have a reading conference with them.

I believe that knowing the levels of understanding can help teachers target their instruction and support students in their ability to move beyond a literal understanding to a deeper and more meaningful reading engagement. I have come to understand that there are three levels of understanding text. At each level, a reader is engaged in a number of different strategies. The chart on page 22 shows the three different levels or layers of understanding. Early in my teaching career, if I had students who were able to read a passage and then retell the beginning, middle, and end of the story with some degree of accuracy, I believed that they had read and understood the text and were ready to move to the next level. Now, having a child simply retell a story is no longer enough. I believe that, in order to fully understand the meaning of a story, readers must interact and interpret the story based on their own experiences and knowledge. Reading Power strategies of connecting, visualizing, questioning, and inferring play a key role in this interactive level of understanding. Ultimately, a reader can take ideas from the text and integrate it with their thinking. This synthesis, or rethinking of a text, is the highest level of understanding. The chart on page 22 is an important reminder that explicit instruction in reading strategies is essential; without it, many of our students will remain in the literal level.

Level 1: Literal
Strategies required: retell, recount, determine importance, summarize

Level 2: Interactive
Strategies required: connect, visualize, question, infer

Level 3: Integrated
Strategies required: transform, synthesize, rethink

Teaching the Reading Powers

The five reading powers do not need to be introduced or taught in any particular order, as they are not dependent on each other. In terms of a hierarchy of skills, however, Inferring and Transforming are definitely more complex—showing integrated understanding—and I recommend not starting with these. Connecting and Visualizing tend to be easiest for the younger students to grasp and are able to be learned and practiced by students who are not yet reading independently.

When deciding which strategies to focus on in which grade, it is important to use reading assessments (formal and informal) from the beginning of the year to learn which strategies your students know and can use at a guided or independent level. Using assessment to guide your instruction supports an approach based on *looking up* at your students, as opposed to *looking down* at your curriculum. Some early primary teachers might decide that they are not going to begin explicit instruction in the strategies until later in the year, while others might discover that their students already know how to make connections, but struggle with inferring. I often begin the year focusing on Making Connections because it can be a way for me to better get to know my students. However, how long I spend on this strategy will depend on the results of their reading assessments.

Using *Reading Power*

Now that the theory and background behind Reading Power is clear, we can focus on the practical application, the *how-to* of explicit teaching of comprehension. There are three important components of Reading Power:

See a more detailed look at the components of Reading Power in chapter 2.

1. Power: The Reading Powers Model (see page 28) represents the metacognitive piece of Reading Power and the importance of providing your students with the "big picture" of what reading and thinking are.
2. Reading Power book collections are a way to organize the literature you will use, and to reinforce the importance of selecting appropriate books to use in modeling, teaching, and practicing the strategies.
3. The Method of Instruction is most important: how to actually teach these strategies in your classroom.

Chapters 3 to 7 will take you deeper into each of the Reading Power strategies. Each of these chapters begins with a song and/or chant to use as a teaching tool, some insight into the strategy, and suggestions on how to introduce the concept to your students. Then a series of teacher-directed and independent lessons follow, taking you through the steps of modeling, guiding, and independent practice, and including suggested book titles for each lesson. You will find student samples, reproducible charts and templates, and an extensive updated lists of recommended anchor books that can be used to teach and practice the strategies, including separate listings of books that reflect aboriginal cultures and that are for older students. Assessment rubrics for each Reading Power strategy are included in each chapter.

Chapter 8: Application and Assessment provides some insight into the importance of the application stage of Reading Power and explores ways to ensure that students are actually applying what they know about reading and thinking to the texts they read independently. It gives instructions on how to integrate the Reading Power strategies into your novel studies or literature circles. As in the preceding chapters, lessons are outlined, and reproducible pages, suggestions for books to use, and assessment rubrics are included. It also looks at home reading and the importance of ensuring your students' parents are aware of this approach., including recommendations on how to involve your parent community. An assessment rubric in child-friendly language is included at the end of this book.

Myths about Reading Power

Thanks to important work in the area of comprehension from such educators as David Pearson, Stephanie Harvey, Debbie Miller, Pat Johnson, Kylene Beers, and Cris Tovani, to name a few, many teachers have made the important shift from "doing" reading with their students to teaching reading. Since *Reading Power* was first published nearly ten years ago, it has grown bigger than I could have ever imagined. Hundreds of teachers across the country have successfully implemented the strategies, modeled their thinking, created book bins, posted the Reading Power model on their classroom walls, and changed the way they implement reading instruction. Children are now using the language of thinking when they read and talk about their reading and engage in more meaningful reading experiences. I have presented dozens of workshops and passionately shared my stories, lessons, books, and ideas. And while I celebrate the enormous growth and change that has occurred in so many classrooms, I have also seen and heard things that significantly stray from my suggestions to improve anyone's teaching practice. I have heard many teachers say, "Well Adrienne says…" when, in fact, I haven't actually said that at all! So I would like to take a moment to clear up some misconceptions that have developed about Reading Power over the years.

Reading Power is a program.
Incorrect. Reading Power is not a "program" that you buy for a large sum, that comes in a box with many different shiny parts. Reading Power is an approach to comprehension instruction that focuses on thinking, metacognition, and explicit instruction.

Reading Power replaces other components of my reading program.
Incorrect. Reading Power is an *addition to*, not *a replacement for*, any part of your reading program. I believe, however, that the strategies students learn from the explicit instruction can be applied to all other aspects of your reading program.

Reading Power is for elementary students.

Incorrect. Reading Power is not limited to any particular grade, but is grounded in the principles of metacognitive awareness and thinking. Over many years of working with teachers, I have seen many middle- and high-school teachers adapt Reading Power lessons for their students, including use of picture books to teach and model the lessons.

I don't have to teach phonics anymore because I teach Reading Power.

Incorrect (with a capital *I*!) Reading Power should not make up your entire reading program. Phonemic and phonological awareness are essential components of a primary reading program and should never be replaced. Reading Power is an addition to, not a replacement of, those skills.

You have to teach the strategies in the order they are found in the book.

Incorrect. The order you teach the strategies matters little to the ultimate goal, which is that your students interact with all the strategies every time they read. Interestingly enough, I have revisited the order in which I introduce or review the strategies since I first started using Reading Power. I now see the value in linking connecting with visualizing, and questioning with inferring, because I have come to better understand how these pairs of strategies merge together in our thinking.

You have to spend two months on each strategy! Adrienne says so!

Incorrect. Depending on your students' previous knowledge and experience with Reading Power, teachers are encouraged to use formative reading assessments and reading conferences to determine what their students know and don't know. If, for example, the majority of your students already know how to make connections, then less time would need to be spent on that one strategy. I initially suggested two months on each strategy if your class had no previous experience with Reading Power strategies. My recommendation is that you put aside two blocks of about 40 minutes each per week for explicit teaching and practicing of the strategies. Use your formative reading assessments at the beginning of the school year to determine which strategies your students already know. You might need to do only one or two review lessons on making connections, for example, but spend more time teaching inferring. Here are some general recommendations:

PHASE 1: INTRODUCING THE READING POWER STRATEGIES

For students who have had NO prior experience in these strategies.

- September/October: Connect (try to integrate both fiction and nonfiction examples into your teaching and modeling)
- November/December: Visualize
- January/February: Question
- March/April: Infer
- May/June: Transform

PHASE 2: APPLICATION OF READING POWER STRATEGIES AND GOING DEEPER

For students who have had previous experience with the strategies

- 2–4 lessons (or longer, depending on results of your reading assessment) reviewing strategy concept using both fiction and nonfiction texts
- Focus on going deeper with the strategies.

- Integrate Reading Power strategies into literature circles or novel study.
- Integrate Reading Power strategies into your teaching of content areas: Math, Science, Social Studies.
- Transfer of learning: students apply all strategies to all books.

You must model your thinking every time you read aloud to your class.
Incorrect. Modeling thinking, while an essential part of the first stage in the gradual-release model (see page 39), takes a lot of time and can be distracting to the story. I most certainly model my thinking when introducing the strategy; I don't model my thinking every time I read to my students. Sometimes, you just need to read, without interruptions, distractions, thinking bubbles, or thumbs up. Just read.

Kindergarten students are too young to learn inferring.
Incorrect. While I would agree that cognitive development does play a factor in a child's ability to fully understand metacognition, I do believe that, with the right book and the right modeling, even young students can learn to infer.

Students can't make connections because they don't have enough experience.
Incorrect. Unfortunately, not all students come to us with rich home-life experiences, leaving some students with less to draw on when making connections. However, while they may not have travelled to Disneyland or skied the Alps, all children have experiences with family, friendship, and feelings, have lost a tooth and have had a birthday. This is why the selection of picture books is so important for helping your students make connections.

If I don't have a book from the list, I can't do the lesson.
Incorrect. I began making book lists to support teachers, as I felt it would be helpful for them to know which books lend themselves best to particular strategies. Ultimately, however, it is my hope that teachers would develop their own lists and use their own understanding of the Reading Power strategies to find their own books to use for modeling and practicing the strategies.

"The good news is that comprehension instruction has become a long overdue reading focus. The bad news is that comprehension strategies and exercises in isolation often dominate comprehension instruction. Students are spending massive amounts of time learning and practicing these strategies, often without knowing how to apply them or not understand how they fit into the big picture of reading."
—Regie Routman, *Reading Essentials*

When I have finished teaching all five Reading Powers, I'm finished!
Incorrect. The strategies are taught in isolation initially so that students develop a strong understanding of each. The goal, however, is that, once you have finished teaching all five, you move into the next phase and start modeling how active readers use all their reading powers when they are reading any book. This stage of application, or transfer of learning, while not an emphasis in my first book, is definitely an important part of this revision.

You need to model your thinking on every page.
Incorrect. Modeling your thinking takes time and can be distracting to the story for some children. I suggest using two or three Read-Aloud/Think-Alouds for introducing a new Reading Power, during which you intentionally stop and share your thinking. I also recommend five or six "thinks" per book—but certainly not one every page. It is important that we provide many opportunities in our classroom for our students to simply savor a story without stopping every two pages to share thinking or ask a question. Sometimes we need to just read. Cynthia Rylant says it best: "Be quiet. Don't talk the experience to death. Shut up and let these kids feel and think."

Reading Power is about reading.
Incorrect. Perhaps this is the biggest misconception of all, and idea I, myself, believed for many years after developing Reading Power. But over the last several years, I have come to realize that Reading Power is not grounded in reading, but in thinking. We think when we read, but we also think when we have conversations, watch movies, listen to music, look at art, do a science experiment. Ultimately, I realized that Reading Power is actually helping students to not only be better readers, but also to be better thinkers.

2   The Components of Reading Power

The Reading Powers Model

Helping Students Become Metacognitive

Good readers have busy brains when they read.

Thinking is an essential part of reading; however, it is an abstract concept and, therefore, difficult to teach. Because we can't "see" thinking, it is difficult for us to describe and explain it. Saying, "Boys and girls, when you read, you need to think" does not really cut it! Young children know that, when they read, they need to be actively using their eyes and often their mouths. But how many of them are aware that their brains also need to be active? It was important that this metacognitive awareness be somehow incorporated into the teaching of Reading Power, so that the students could have a concrete visual image of what needs to be going on inside their heads as they read.

Students will see that the brain becomes filled as their metacognitive knowledge of their thinking develops, demonstrating that active readers have many different things going on their heads while they read.

The Reading Powers Model is an interactive, visual prompt for the during-reading process; see page 28. Each poster depicts a child's head and shoulders, and the phrase "Fill Your Brain with Reading Power!" at the top. There are five separate, removable puzzle pieces that fit together and can be superimposed on the child's head. Each piece is labeled with a different reading power. As each reading power is introduced and taught, the appropriate puzzle piece is placed inside the image of the child's head. The idea behind the puzzle is that the pieces fit together to create the ideal proficient reader—"A POWER-ful brain reads well."

Because proficient readers often move from one strategy to another within a single reading experience, it is important to teach these reading powers cumulatively rather than separately. New pieces are added as new reading powers are introduced, but the pieces are never removed once placed in the head.

What Does Thinking Look Like?

With younger children, I sometimes introduce the Reading Power Model by asking, "What parts of your body do you use when you read?" They often answer "hands" first, for holding the book. Other answers quickly follow: mouth, eyes, ears. But "the brain" is not an answer very often given, because we don't often refer to the brain when we are teaching students how to read.

Early in the school year, I like to explain to my students that one of my goals for them is that they will all be better readers in June than they are in September. The way I hope to reach this goal is by giving them many opportunities to read, but also by teaching them ways they can become more proficient readers. I explain that reading happens in two places: in the book and in your head. It happens in the book when we focus on the words with our eyes; it happens in our brains when we focus on what the words mean with our brains. Depending on the grade, I will say that most have them have already learned the in-the-book reading because they know how to read the words. I explain that, for the upcoming year, the focus of some of the reading lessons will be on the in-your-head reading.

The Reading Powers Model

Name: _____   Date: _____

Fill Your Brain with Reading Power!

- Begin the lesson by telling students that you will be spending a few minutes talking about the *thinking* part of reading. Ask them to have a pencil and a paper ready to do a short exercise. When students are ready, tell them they have 15 seconds to draw a picture of an apple. After 15 seconds, tell them to put their pencils down and to share and compare their apple drawing with a partner.
- Ask class questions about their drawings: *Who had a round apple? Curved apple? Stem? Leaf? Shiny spot?* etc.
- Ask students if it was easy or hard to draw a picture of an apple (*Easy!*) Why? (*Because we know what one looks like, have seen one, eaten one, touched one, etc.*)
- Tell students they have 15 seconds to draw a picture of *thinking*. After 15 seconds, invite students to share and compare.
- Many children will draw thought bubbles like the ones shown in comics or cartoons. Explain that a thought bubble shows thinking happening in the air, but that thinking actually happens in their heads.
- Invite students to revise their thinking pictures to show thinking happening on the inside of their heads. Have them share and compare their thinking pictures with a partner.
- Discuss the difference between drawing a picture of an apple and drawing a picture of thinking. Which was more challenging? (*Thinking*) Why? (*Because we can't see it.*)
- Explain to students that thinking is a very important part of reading, but that it is difficult to teach thinking since we can't actually see it! Ask, "What does thinking look like?"
- Tell the students that you have something that can help answer the question.

Grade 2 Sample

I encourage teachers to name their model or have students help come up with a name for it. I call my Reading Powers Model Howard.

Introducing the Thinking Brain

- Bring out the Reading Powers Model (see page 28) and explain to the students that Howard is a good reader who uses his eyes to read the words and his brain to think about those words. He is going to help us answer the question *What does thinking look like?* With the puzzle pieces in hand, I introduce, in brief, each of the reading powers, to help the students to "see thinking" more clearly:

I have very young children use magical "X-ray glasses" so they can look inside Howard's brain and watch while the pieces are placed inside.

The reason I know Howard is a good reader is that when he reads, his brain is busy. And if we could look inside Howard's head while he was reading, we would see five things going on in there. We call these five things "reading powers" because they've helped Howard become a powerful reader. Let's look inside Howard's brain to see what exactly is going on in there when he reads.

One way Howard uses his brain to think about a story is called *Connecting*. That means that something Howard might be reading about reminds him of something that happened to him once. Or he might be reading about a character that reminds him of himself or someone he knows. Or he might be reading a book that reminds him of another book he's read. And when that happens, it's called a *connection*.

(Place *Connect* piece in head.)

Howard is reading chapter books and novels, and most of these books do not have pictures in them. But Howard can read a story and, while he's reading, he can make the pictures right in his head. It's not a picture he sees with his eyes, but a picture he sees in his brain—a thinking picture. That is called *Visualizing*, and active readers visualize when they read to help them think about the story.

(Place *Visualize* piece in head.)

Another way Howard thinks about what he reads is to ask *Questions*. Sometimes teachers ask him questions after he's finished reading, but active readers ask questions *while* they read. Howard wonders while he reads.

(Place *Question* piece in head.)

Another thing that this reader can do while he reading and thinking is called *Inferring*. That might be a word that you have never heard before, but good readers infer while they read. This reader knows that not all authors write everything down in words. Some authors leave clues in their pictures and stories, and it's up to Howard to try to figure out what the author is trying to say. It's like he's filling in, in his head, what is not written on the page. After he asks a question he might try to answer it by adding a "maybe" into the story.

(Place *Infer* piece in head.)

The last thing that happens to Howard when he reads certain books is that his thinking is *Transformed*. That doesn't mean he turns into a robot or a building, but it does mean that some changes happen inside his head. You might read a story and say to yourself *"Hmm... I have never thought about it that way before."* To transform is to change, and sometimes Howard's thinking changes while he's reading.

(Place *Transform* piece in head.)

(Hold an open book up to the Reading Powers Model.)

Let's watch Howard read for a while. Oh... Howard just made a connection. Now he's wondering something.... Now he's visualizing.... Now he's making another connection…. Now he's inferring…. Wow! Howard's brain is certainly busy, isn't it? He's using the all the reading powers, and you can too. Each reading power is a piece of your thinking that can help you understand what you read.

Howard has been reading this way for a long time, he's able to use the reading powers at the same time. He goes back and forth between them while he's reading—on one page he might ask a question, on the next page he might make a connection, then on another page he might make a picture in his head. But it's a little hard to do them all at once, so this year we are going to learn them one at a time. And I'll tell you something that might surprise you—you have all of these reading powers in your brains already, you just might not know it!

Children have often laughed at Howard, calling him Rainbow Brain and Helmet Head, but the Reading Powers Model has provided them with a visual that they might not otherwise have. At my school, this visual has been the focal point for many children's conversations. One class may join another class for buddy reading and recognize the Model, but see a different piece inside the head. The Reading Powers Model can help reinforce the common language of thinking and help turn an abstract concept into something concrete.

Each time I begin a new reading power, I always go back to Howard and review the idea of what thinking looks like with my students:

Why are we learning this again? We are learning this because good readers think while they read, and this thinking helps them understand the story better. Thinking looks different to every person because each of us has different ideas and experiences stored in our heads. But if we all learn to use our thinking brains by making connections or asking questions or making pictures in our heads, we will learn to how to understand the story better.

Over the years, there have been many adaptations to the Reading Powers Model. Some teachers use store-bought posters of celebrities and place the brain pieces directly on the posters. Some primary teachers, who might not be teaching all the reading powers, have adapted the brain pieces by enlarging three of them to fit inside the head rather than using all five. Some intermediate teachers have had their classes design their own Models, in which they include unique hairstyles, clothes, and even face piercings! I know of a principal who told me he doesn't use the poster anymore: "I'm large, I'm bald—so I just stick the pieces on my head!" How you develop or create the Model is up to you, but I do believe it is essential to create a concrete visual for you and your students to refer to: *This is what thinking looks like.*

Students at Gitwinksihlkw Elementary School (School District 92 Nisga'a in the Nass Valley north of Terrace, BC) display their "personalized" Reading Power brains!

The Reading Power Theme Song

Connect Song: page 43
Visualize Song and Chant: page 67
Question Song: page 89
Infer Song: page 108
Transform Song and Chant: page 128

After the introduction lesson, the students of Tina Gill's Kindergarten class created the Reading Power Theme Song (below) and sang it for me, shouting the word "Brain" each time they sang it. Having five-year-olds sing a song about metacognition was most inspiring! I asked them why they were shouting the word "Brain" in the song, and one boy told me that it was "because the brain is so important when you read!" When I began teaching Reading Power to the intermediate students, I borrowed Mrs. Gill's Kindergarten class to sing the song to the bigger kids.

Mrs. Gill's class inspired me to create a song or chant to accompany each of the reading powers. They can be taught as you introduce a new reading power and will help to reinforce the key ideas for each strategy. As my own class helped me write many of the verses, feel free to replace or add your own. I know of schools in Vancouver where they are reinforcing the common language throughout the school through these songs, singing the songs at weekly school assemblies as the school focuses on each of the strategies.

* * *

Reading Power Theme Song
(to the tune of "Head & Shoulders")

A more hygienic trend is to give a fist-bump instead of a high-five. You can change the lyrics to reflect this.

Hands and mouth and
Eyes and BRAIN!
Eyes and BRAIN!
Eyes and BRAIN!
Hands and mouth and
Eyes and BRAIN!
High-five Reading Power!

Reading Power Book Collections

"For the price of a bowl of soup, I bought today at an old bookshop a volume infinitely valuable. All the way home on the train I read it; I was enlarged, I acquired merit, I added to my life."
—David Grayson

On the first day of my Language Arts methodology course at the University of British Columbia many years ago, the professor, a woman by the name of Clare Staubs, entered the small room in the Ponderosa Building and began her lecture by reading aloud the first chapter of *The Great Gilly Hopkins* by Katherine Patterson. She told us, on that first day, that the single most important thing that we could do as teachers was to read aloud to our students every day. She began every lecture after that by reading another chapter from the book and, while some in her class may have been put off by her read-alouds during a university class, I was forever changed. That experience had perhaps a more profound impact on me as a teacher than anything else I learned. I made a commitment to myself that, when I became a teacher, I was going to do just what Clare Staubs suggested. In my more than twenty years of teaching, I have made many mistakes, but reading aloud to my class every day was something I have been committed to and never regretted. No matter what the grade, no matter what was going on in the day, I read aloud to my students every day they walk into my classroom. Reading aloud to students every day is my responsibility as a teacher, but for me it has also been a privilege. The literature that is available to children, teens, and young adults now is so extraordinarily rich, stunningly beautiful, and profound that we would be doing our students an enormous disservice if we did not share it with them. Books have "added to my life," as David Grayson puts it, and have certainly added to the lives of my students.

I encourage intermediate teachers to use picture books in their classrooms when introducing each of the strategies. David Pearson speaks about how he believes that, if teachers continue to try to teach students new reading strategies using texts that are "at the edge of their competence," students will have a much more difficult time grasping the new strategy and applying it to their reading; whereas if we bring the reading level down slightly to teach and practice the strategy, the students will have a far easier time learning and applying it. This supports my belief that using picture books that are at a slightly less challenging reading level to teach a strategy gives our students a better chance of seeing, learning, and understanding the strategy. Intermediate children are thrilled to be given permission to read picture books, and enjoy the experience tremendously. I have had Grade 7 students fight over who gets *No, David!* books by David Shannon to practice Connecting, or leaping up to grab *The Cinder-Eyed Cats* for Visualizing.

Reading Power opens the door to literature for both teachers and students, and introduces them to an extraordinary range of titles, authors, and illustrators. Once I became familiar with the type of books that support each strategy, it became difficult to read a new book without thinking about which strategy I might use it for. During workshops, teachers often tell me of books they know that are not on the list that would be "perfect for Connecting" or "perfect for Visualizing." I encourage you to add your own favorites to the lists in this book. Certain books just lend themselves well to a certain strategy, and it is obvious how to categorize them. Other books tend to fit more than one strategy. I know a book is good when I don't know what bin to put it in!

In as much as I am committed to read aloud every day, I must admit that at times there used to be no rhyme or reason for my daily read-alouds. I often just read a book to my students because I liked it, it suited the special occasion of the calendar year, or I had had a recent visit to a bookstore. But now, Reading Power has given me the structure under which all my read-alouds now fall. I specifically choose books that support the strategy I am teaching and intentionally integrate the language while I read. It is for this reason that I created Reading Power book bins. The book bins are not a necessity and, let's face it, can be an expensive endeavor, but they have made life a little easier for the teachers who use them. There is not enough time in a teacher's day, and having all the books in one place, ready to go, has certainly proved to be a huge time saver.

I love picture books, but have discovered over the years that some books just work better for teaching and practicing a strategy than others. I decided to create Reading Power book bins that each contains a collection of books specifically selected because they lend themselves best to a particular strategy. Books are stored in a plastic tub to be signed out by teachers. Some schools keep the book tubs in the library, while others store their books in their classrooms.

"Great books are central to teaching comprehension."
—Harvey & Goudvis, *Strategies That Work*

Connect Books: page 55
Visualize Books: page 77
Question Books: page 99
Infer Books: page 118
Transform Books: page 140
Novel Study Books: page 168

Picture books are not just for use in primary grades. In fact, many of the picture books available now I would consider too challenging both in language and theme for younger students.

Some teachers select three or four books for each strategy that they keep separately. These Gem Books are used by the teachers specifically for their modeling lessons.

"Close reading does not happen when you read x number of times. It happens when what you are reading matters to you."
—Kyleen Beers, *Notice and Note*

We all experience frustration when a student announces, "We read that book last year!" just as you begin to read. While we cannot prevent this from happening, we can find ways to reduce this problem by designating certain books for certain grades. This requires some negotiating and collaboration among teachers, and possibly the storing of specific books for modeling lessons separately. Another way to avoid repeat reads is to rotate the Reading Power books each year. As new books are purchased and placed into tubs, some of the older titles can be added to the school library collection. Some teacher librarians label these books on the spine with a *C, V, Q, I,* or *T* so that they can be easily found on the shelves.

The turnover of children's books is enormous and, as one title goes out of print, there are three more great new titles released. After conferring with several teacher-librarians in the district, I have decided to keep some books that have gone out of print on this list. Some of these out-of-print books are classics and there always seems to be copies of them hiding on library shelves, waiting to be read.

Here are lists of my top picks, favorite new books for both Primary and Intermediate grades for each of the five reading powers. If a school is creating a Reading Power collection, these would be the books I would purchase as a starter collection. More extensive lists are included at the end of each strategy chapter. I am thrilled with the quality of extraordinary picture books I have been able to share in these lists and that you, in turn, can share with your students.

Reading Power Books

CONNECT (PRIMARY)

Anholt, Catherine & Laurence. *Good Days, Bad Days*
Carlson, Nancy. *Sometimes You Barf*
Curtis, Jamie. *My Brave Book of Firsts*
Juster, Norton. *The Hello, Goodbye Window*
McBratney, Sam. *I'm Sorry*
Parr, Todd. *It's Okay to Make Mistakes*
Rosenthal, Amy Krouse. *The OK Book*
Schwartz, Amy. *100 Things That Make Me Happy*
Shannon, David. *No, David!* (or any of the David books)
Shannon, David. *Too Many Toys!*
Stinson, Kathy. *Red is Best*
Young, Jessica. *My Blue Is Happy*

CONNECT (INTERMEDIATE)

Boelts, Maribeth. *Those Shoes*
Browne, Anthony. *What If?*
Fleischman, Paul. *Matchbox Diary*
Heide, Florence Parry. *Some Things Are Scary*
Kelly, Marty. *12 Terrible Things*
Khan, Rukhsana. *Big Red Lollipop*
Larsen, Andrew. *See You Next Year*
O'Neill, Alexis. *The Worst Best Friend*
Polacco, Patricia. *Bully*
Rapp, Jennifer. *I Can Wait for the Bell to Ring*

Rosenthal, Amy Krouse. *One of Those Days*
Waber, Bernard. *Courage*

VISUALIZE (PRIMARY)

Ets, Marie Hall. *Gilberto and the Wind*
Keats, Ezra Jack. *The Snowy Day*
Lemniscates. *Silence*
London, Jonathan. *Puddles*
Morris, Jackie. *Tell Me A Dragon*
Pendziwol, Jean E. *Once Upon a Northern Night*
Weiss, George David & Bob Thiele. *What a Wonderful World*
Willis, Jeanne. *Mole's Sunrise*
Yankey, Lindsay. *Bluebird*

VISUALIZE (INTERMEDIATE)

Carroll, Lewis; James A. Stewart (illus.). *Jabberwocky*
Cooper, Elisha. *A Good Night Walk*
Cottin, Menena. *The Black Book of Color*
Larsen, Andrew. *See You Next Year*
Noyes, Alfred; Murray Kimber (illus.). *The Highwayman*
Pilkey, Dav. *The Paperboy*
Reid, Barbara. *Snow Day*
Ryan, Pam Munoz. *Hello, Ocean*
Van Dusan, Chris. *If I Built a House*

QUESTION (PRIMARY)

Barnett, Mac. *Sam and Dave Dig a Hole*
Bunting, Eve. *Fly Away Home*
Campbell, K.G. *The Mermaid and the Shoe*
Nelson, Kadir. *Baby Bear*
Rohmann, Eric. *The Cinder-Eyed Cats*
Santat, Dan. *The Adventures of Beekle*
Soman, David. *Three Bears in a Boat*
Stinson, Kathy. *The Man and the Violin*

QUESTION (INTERMEDIATE)

Abercrombie, Barbara. *Charlie Anderson*
Adderson, Caroline. *Norman, Speak!*
Bunting, Eve. *Smoky Nights*
Davies, Nicola. *The Promise*
Gallaz, Christophe. *Rose Blanche*
Lauthier, Jennifer. *The Stamp Collector*
De Lestrade, Agnes. *Phileas's Fortune*
Miki, Roy & Slavia. *Dolphin SOS*
Pennypacker, Sara. *Sparrow Girl*
Perry, Sarah. *If*
Say, Allen. *The Stranger in the Mirror*
Skarmeta, Antonio. *The Composition*
Wild, Margaret. *Fox*

INFER (PRIMARY)

Alborough, Jez. *Hug*
Boyd, Lizi. *Inside Outside*
Boyd, Lizi. *The Farmer and the Clown*
Lee, JiHyeon. *Pool*
Lehman, Barbara. *The Red Book* (or *The Museum Trip*)
Mack, Jeff. *Look!*
Meyer, Mercer. *A Boy, a Dog, and a Frog*
Miyares, Daniel. *Float*
Pett, Mark. *The Girl and the Bicycle* (or *The Boy and the Airplane*)
Thomson, Bill. *Chalk* (or *Fossil*)
Van Hout, Mies. *Happy*
Young, Cybele. *Ten Birds*

INFER (INTERMEDIATE)

Aslan, Christopher. *Dude*

Baker, Jeannie. *Window*
Baker, Jeannie. *Mirror*
Browne, Anthony. *Voices in the Park* (or *Zoo*, or any of his books)
Lawson, JonArno .*Sidewalk Flowers*
Lee, JiHyeon. *Pool*
Popov, *Why?*
Raschka, Chris. *Yo! Yes!*
Tan, Sean. *Rules of Summer*
Van Allsburg, Chris. Any of his books; *The Stranger*, *The Sweetest Fig*, and *Mysteries of Harris Burdick* are my favorites
Wiesner, David. *Flotsam*
Willis, Jeanne. *Chicken Clicking*
Young, Cybele. *The Queen's Shadow*

TRANSFORM (PRIMARY)

Barnett, Mac. *Extra Yarn*
Brown, Peter. *Mr. Tiger Goes Wild*
Cousins, Lucy. *I'm the Best!*
DiOrio, Rana. *What Does It Need to Be Present?*
Hall, Michael. *Red: A Crayon's Story*
Johnson, Mariana Ruiz. *I Know a Bear*
Nelson, Kadir. *If You Plant a Seed*
Pearson, Emily. *Ordinary Mary's Extraordinary Deed*
Snicket, Lemony. *The Dark*
Spires, Ashley. *The Most Magnificent Thing*
Upjohn, Rebecca. *Lily and the Paper Man*

TRANSFORM (INTERMEDIATE)

Brisson, Pat. *Melissa Parkington's Beautiful, Beautiful Hair*
Bunting, Eve. *Yard Sale*
Danneberg, Julie. *First Day Jitters*
De Kinder, Jan. *Red*
Ludwig, Trudy. *The Invisible Boy*
Madonna. *Mr. Peabody's Apple*
Rath, Tom. *How Full is Your Bucket? For Kids*
Reynolds, Peter H. *Ish*
Tsuchiya, Yukio. *Faithful Elephants*
Zuckerberg, Randi. *Dot*

Creating a Reading Power Book Collection

The success of this program is not tied to the specific book titles provided; it is grounded in the principles of thinking. I always stress in workshops that creating Reading Power book collections for your school is not a necessity; however, it does make things easier.

I have heard on more than one occasion, "Oh, I can't do that lesson because I don't have that book." As teachers, most of us have our own collection of books that accumulate in our classroom each year. Reading Power collections can begin simply with your personal collection. I encourage you to use the books you already have before going out and spending a fortune on new books. School and local libraries are also invaluable resources for gathering material for your modeling lessons. Here are some general guidelines I use when sorting books to use for different strategies:

- Connect Books: family, friendship, feelings, school, siblings, losing a tooth, holidays
- Visualize Books: descriptive, poetry, seasons, weather, places
- Question Books: poverty, homelessness, war, friendship issues, historical fiction, fantasy
- Infer Books: wordless picture books, books with very little text
- Transform Books: war, peace, homelessness, kindness, making a difference, taking risks, social responsibility

Part of what makes Reading Power unique among approaches to comprehension instruction is its tie to high-quality children's literature; part of what makes Reading Power unique to individual teachers is the books they choose for modeling and practicing with their students. Teachers will need to look for the most appropriate books for their particular school culture—as well as for the age and interests of their students—to add to their own Reading Power book collections. Adding your own favorites to your collection will increase your and your students' interest and understanding of each Reading Power.

To get started on your collection, here are some tips:

- Purchase sturdy plastic tubs for storing the books. I like to use clear ones so the titles are visible from the outside. I prefer to store the books vertically rather than flat so that I can flip through and see the titles more easily. Have one tub for each Reading Power strategy. Label each book with the strategy so they can be easily replaced in the appropriate tub.
- Use the lists at the end of each section as your starting point. You DO NOT need to purchase all the books on the list, but try to select a few from each heading (theme) to ensure a variety of topics in each bin.
- Books for Modeling (Gems): three to four books for each reading power to be used by teachers only
- Books for Independent Practice: ideally enough for one per student or one for each pair of students (15–30 books)
- Create separate Primary and Intermediate collections.
- These books should not be leveled, but should include books for a range of reading abilities.
- One tub of books costs between $300 and $400, depending on how smart a shopper you are and if the books are hard or soft cover.
- Each bin should have a list of books inside—taped to the inside cover or loose in the bottom of the bin—so that teachers can do a quick inventory before returning or passing it on to another teacher.
- Bins should be kept in a central location with some type of sign-out system, so that teachers know where to find them.

If your school does decide to create Reading Power book collections, here are some suggestions of ways to find the best sources in your area:

- Scholastic Book Fairs and monthly Book Clubs
- Public libraries often hold yearly book sales where you can get picture books in decent condition for very reasonable prices.
- Local bookstores—whenever possible, support your local independent bookstores.
- Used bookstores—always treasures waiting to be discovered!
- Chapters.Indigo.ca, Amazon.com, Barnesandnoble.com, etc.
- Flea markets and garage sales
- Google search for used bookstores if you are looking for a particular title (www.alibris.com or www.abebooks.com are both great resources for finding used books).
- Don't forget garage and church sales, local bookstores, and warehouse sales in larger centres.

If your school decides not to create Reading Power book collections, here are some alternatives:

- Visit your school library or your local library with a book list in hand. Focus on taking out books connected to one strategy at a time.
- Have a teacher-librarian pull the books and create shelves for each Reading Power strategy.
- Have a teacher-librarian label the spines of appropriate books with *C, V, Q, I,* and/or *T* for each reading power, so that teachers and students can locate them quickly.
- Use your own classroom book collection and label the appropriate books with the Reading Power strategy.

Reading Power Instruction

Modeling

I always tell teachers at my workshops that they don't really need the Reading Powers Model and don't really need Reading Power book bins. What is essential to the success of this program is ongoing explicit and direct teaching of comprehension strategies.

We can never assume that students comprehend their own inner voice of understanding. The Reading Powers Model helps answer the question *What does thinking look like?*, but only the teacher can help answer the question *What does thinking sound like?* If we want to help our students become better readers, we need to show them what a good reader looks like, sounds like, and thinks like (Stephanie Harvey demonstrates this brilliantly in her videos; many samples of teacher modeling can be found on YouTube). I try to model it when I give workshops. I don't find it difficult to do, and some teachers are more comfortable doing it than others, but once students see and hear their teacher reading out loud and thinking out loud, comprehension becomes a tangible, concrete experience for them.

I went to university at a time when Whole Language was the rage. I learned to become a "facilitator" and an "observer" in the classroom. I learned how to assess using a variety of checklists and how to meet the needs of my students by working with small groups and teaching on an "as the need arises" basis. I don't

One of Richard Allington's 6 T's of Effective Literacy Instruction includes teacher modeling: "Teacher consistently provides direct, explicit modeling of cognitive strategies used by readers to engage in text."

Teachers have many opportunities in their day to model their thinking. It does not need to be in a formal lesson—I encourage you to find moments in your everyday conversations, read-alouds, whole-class reading, or guided reading when you can stop and model your thinking.

remember learning how to do a great deal of direct teaching, nor do I remember having sponsor teachers who did a lot of explicit instruction.

When I taught my five-year-old son how to tie his shoe laces, I did not do it by telling him how. I *showed* him how—not just once, but many, many times. Then he tried to do it himself and he practiced—not just once, but many, many times. A new skill, whether it be tying shoes or reading with meaning, needs to be taught in the same way.

I explain to my students:

> We have two voices: a speaking voice and a thinking voice. A speaking voice is the voice people hear when we talk. A thinking voice is the voice inside our heads that other people can't hear. When we read silently and our speaking voice is quiet, our thinking voice needs to be very, very loud.

Thinking needs to be made visible and concrete, and there are different ways to illustrate this. Sticky notes stuck directly on the pages while you read can mark your "thinking voice." John Dyer, a primary teacher in Vancouver, has a wonderful method of showing his students when he is using his thinking voice. He attaches a large white cutouts of a Talking bubble and a Thinking bubble to rulers (see templates on page 42). Each time he reads from a book with his speaking voice, he holds up the Talking bubble. Each time he is explaining what his thinking voice is saying, he switches and holds up his Thinking bubble.

It is that thinking voice that helps a reader make sense of what they are reading. During all the modeling lessons in which I first introduce a new strategy, I explain to the students exactly what I am going to be doing:

> Today I'm going to be reading this story out loud and using my speaking voice. But every time my thinking voice makes a connection (or asks a question, or makes a picture in my head, etc.) I'm going to stop reading and tell you what I'm thinking. It is called a "read-aloud/think-aloud."

I have had teachers tell me that these read-aloud/think-alouds take a long time. Yes, they do. They take much longer than simply reading a story. But I strongly believe that it is time well spent. It is important to take this time when introducing a strategy. Remind yourself that you are not going to be reading aloud this way forever—you are simply showing your students how to "tie their shoelaces." If you don't show them, they will eventually trip over the pages of their texts with little or no understanding.

Some teachers have expressed concern over the "distraction" this can cause to their reading. Is it distracting to have to stop every few pages to tell your class what you are thinking about? Yes, it can be. But remember the point of the lesson. It is not my intention to ask students questions about the content of the text after I finish reading: the intention of this lesson is to model my thinking.

Once students see what you are doing, they inevitably want to participate. This will end up taking too much time. It is important for students to know that, while you are modeling, it is your turn:

> For the next few days I'm going to be *modeling my thinking*. When I'm modeling, it means that it is my turn to share my thinking voice.

"I argue with myself, you're telling stories and you're supposed to be teaching. I am teaching. Storytelling is teaching."
—Frank McCourt, *Teacher Man*

I know that I won't be "reading and thinking" in this manner for every read-aloud, but it is important that students hear what thinking sounds like when I introduce them to a new strategy.

"Oh, I get it! It's like reading on the inside!"
—Grade 5 student

One way we solved this problem was the "quiet connections thumbs-up" system—if children make a connection while you're reading, they can participate by showing you their thumbs-up without interrupting your modeling lesson. This works for the most part, except for the occasional student who continues to wave double thumbs up in huge circles in front of your face while you read! A teacher told me at a workshop that she was substituting in a Kindergarten class and, while she was reading, the students all started making strange "donkey ear" gestures on their heads. Surprised by this strange reaction, she asked them what they were doing. "We're making connections," one student explained. "This is our brain moving!"

Components of Reading Instruction

1. **Explanation of the strategy**
2. **Teacher Modeling**: explicit teaching, demonstrating, reading aloud/thinking aloud, "thinking voice–speaking voice"
3. **Guided Practice**: teacher and students practicing together in large or small groups
4. **Independent Practice**: students applying the strategy on their own, with monitoring
5. **Application** to real reading and writing experiences

"Reading aloud with children is known to be the single most important activity for building the knowledge and skills they will eventually require for learning to read."
—Marilyn Jager Adams

The chart above outlines the Components of Reading Instruction based on the Gradual Release of Responsibility Model (Pearson and Gallagher, 1983), or the more common I do/We do/You do model. Interestingly, in the first edition of this book, I focused on the importance of the Teacher Modeling stage. At that time, teacher modeling was a fairly new concept for me. I believed then, as I do now, that repeated modeling of your thinking while you read aloud to your students is a critical component of comprehension instruction. We should never assume that children have ever heard "that voice" inside their heads while they read, and they need to see and hear our inner voices while we read in order to be able to activate their own. I believe teachers have come to understand the importance and value of modeling their thinking and gave made this an integral part of their reading instruction: read-aloud/think-aloud has become common practice in many classrooms; numerous YouTube clips of teachers modeling their thinking can be viewed; thinking-bubbles cutouts can be seen popping up above teachers' heads.

Regularly and intentionally integrating the language of thinking into your classroom is essential to helping your students understand more clearly that these strategies are intended for every reading experience and with any text.

Teachers will often ask, "How many times do I need to model?" When you are first introducing the reading powers, it is essential that you model your thinking explicitly with at least two or three different books over two or three different days. After that, continue to model your thinking when you read, but not to the extent that you would during those first introductory lessons, pausing only once or twice to share your thinking, rather than throughout the book.

I remember clearly the first year I was teaching Reading Power. I had been modeling Connecting for several weeks. The children were very polite as I paused repeatedly during my lengthy read-alouds to share the parts of my life that the story reminded me of. After several days and many modeling lessons, little Christian put up his hand and said, "Uh, Miss Gear—we get it." Perhaps I had made the gradual release of responsibility a little too gradual, but I would rather have one *we get it* than twenty *I don't get it*s.

In the second stage, Guided Practice, students need time to work in a whole-class or small-group setting, with the teacher still guiding them and using the language of the strategy. These strategies can also be reinforced during your guided reading lessons. During the guided practice stage, it is important for teachers to provide opportunities for students to share their thinking with each other. Discussion helps children sort out their ideas and strengthens their understanding, helping to make their ideas more concrete. Understanding evolves from conversation.

In the Independent Practice stage, the children are ready to work through the strategy on their own with their own book. I read a blog post recently by the late Grant Wiggins, co-founder of the ground-breaking Understanding By Design. In it, he wrote about how far we have come in strategy instruction and the noticeable success of the gradual-release model and teacher modeling. He went on to say, however, that the one area of the gradual-release model we seem to be falling short on is step 4: Independent Practice. He refers to this stage as the "successful transfer of learning for comprehension," where students are fluent, self-regulating, and selecting from a repertoire of strategies. However, teachers aren't doing enough, in his opinion, to support this transfer of understanding.

Finally, our goal for anything we teach is that the students will be able to apply what they learn in all reading situations. This stage is likely the most important one, but perhaps is emphasized the least. While natural to do so, we cannot assume that once students learn a strategy and practice connecting with a connect book that they will turn around and apply the strategy the next day during their read-to-self. I recall that Carmen, a Grade 3 student who had been working on making connections in her class, asked me, "Ms. Gear, am I allowed to make a connection with a library book?" While we may chuckle at this comment, this child clearly had not transferred her understanding from a lesson to her independent reading. Clearly, she hadn't grasped the concept of Application! (I explore this important stage in more detail in chapter 8.)

Components of Reading Power Instruction

Because of the importance of explicit teaching in this approach, I have used it as a framework to present a general outline of what Reading Power instruction might look like in a classroom

1. Teacher Modeling (week 1)

- Introduce and explain the new reading power strategy. Refer back to the Reading Powers Model (page 28) to emphasize and remind students the objective of becoming good readers.
- Use the phrase "good readers" as much as possible for each specific reading power.
- From the recommended books, select one anchor book per day for two to three days (depending on the grade and students' experience with the strategy) for your modeling.
- Read the anchor book: as you read, stop and share your thinking aloud.
- Use sticky notes or cardboard "thinking bubbles" to share your thoughts, connections, questions, etc., sticking them directly into the book wherever you stop.

When teaching a child to ride a bicycle, we hold on to the bike and run alongside, giving the child tips and encouragement. This stage of the gradual-release model is like that, as we run alongside our students and help them gain confidence.

"Conversation is a basis for critical thinking. It is the thread that ties together cognitive strategies and provides students with the practice that becomes the foundation for reading, writing, and thinking."
—Ann Ketch, *The Reading Teacher*

Effective teachers of reading comprehension help their students develop into strategic, active readers, in part, by teaching them why, how, and when to apply certain strategies shown to be used by effective readers. (Duke & Pearson, 2002)

2. Guided Practice (week 2)

- Select a book from the collection to use in guided practice in a whole class or small group. Read the story aloud, but instead of sharing your thinking, invite the students to share theirs.
- Pass out sticky notes or individual thinking bubbles and, as you read, ask for students to come up and stick their notes in the book (or hold up their individual thinking bubbles) to indicate connections, questions, etc.
- Use the language of the strategy wherever possible.
- Support students, giving feedback and encouraging discussions.
- Provide opportunities for students to share their thinking with each other.
- Reinforce strategy during guided reading lessons.

3. Independent Practice (weeks 3–4)

- It is very important to continue modeling and guided practice each day.
- Individually or in pairs, students practice the reading power with sticky notes and books from the collection.
- Sometimes students read-aloud/think-aloud with a partner; other times they read-silently/think-on-paper solo, then share with a partner (this works well with Daily 5 choices).
- Come together to discuss and share ideas as a group or during individual conferences.
- Students can make their own charts, respond in journals or response logs, or use response sheets you provide to extend their thinking into writing.
- Create an anchor chart with some thinking prompts for different strategies and have it visible in the classroom.
- Use thinking prompts from the box below to create a metacognition anchor chart to display in your class. These prompts could also be used to create Thinking bookmarks for students to keep in their independent reading books.

Metacognition Thinking Prompts

- I'm thinking…
- I'm wondering…
- I'm noticing…
- I'm picturing…
- It reminds me of…
- Maybe…
- I never thought about…
- I just learned …

Think about your thinking!

Individual thinking bubbles can be made by attaching a small cardboard cutout thinking bubble to a craft stick.

Talking and Thinking Bubble Templates

Name: _____   Date: _____

Talking

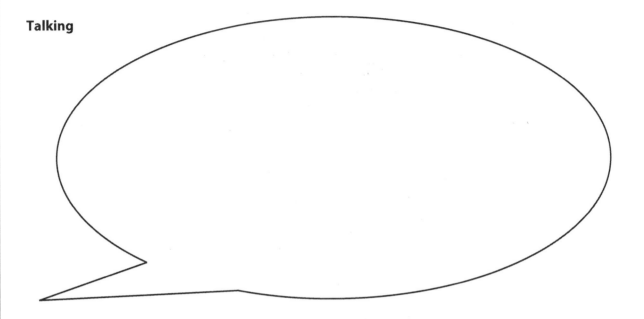

Thinking

Pembroke Publishers © 2015 *Reading Power, Revised and Expanded* by Adrienne Gear ISBN 978-1-55138-310-1

3 The Power to Connect

Connect Song
(to the tune of "Brush Your Teeth")

When I read a story and my brain says, "Hey!
This part reminds me of the other day!"
It's called "connect"—da da da da da da da da da da
It's called "connect"—da da da da da da da da da da

When I read a story and my brain says, "Whoa!
This part reminds me of my friend, Jo!"
It's called "connect"—da da da da da da da da da da
It's called "connect"—da da da da da da da da da da

When I read a story and my brain says, "Cool!
This part reminds me of my school!"
It's called "connect"—da da da da da da da da da da
It's called "connect"—da da da da da da da da da da

When I read a story and my brain says "Look!
This part reminds me of another book!"
It's called "connect"—da da da da da da da da da da
It's called "connect"—da da da da da da da da da da

When I read a story and my brain says, "Wow!
This part reminds me of my grandpa's cow!"
It's called "connect"—da da da da da da da da da da
It's called "connect"—da da da da da da da da da da

* * *

"No story sits by itself. Sometimes stories meet at corners and sometimes they cover one another like stones beneath a river."
—Mitch Albom, *The Five People You Meet in Heaven*

I am in a book club. At the end of our monthly meetings, after rich and thoughtful discussions about the books, after sharing passages that affected us or images that stayed with us, after analyzing the writers' craft, there are some books I may "accidentally" leave behind at the host's house. Other books I bring home, but then happily pass on to my sister or a friend to read without worrying about getting them back. But there are a certain few books I bring home from book club and place on a special shelf on the bookcase in my living room. There they are, not to be read by anyone else, but to sit and be coveted. I touch their spines every once in a while—I may even flip through the pages—but those books have become my treasures. Why, I often wondered, did some books end up on this shelf and not others? Children often say they like a particular book because "it was good." Perhaps that actually means, "I connected to this book." I now understand that the books that end up on my shelf are there because my life story has somehow been woven into their pages. Those books are no longer someone else's story—they have become my story.

The ability to connect to text is perhaps the easiest one for children to understand and master, yet it is singularly the most powerful. Connecting creates the path for all other reading strategies to walk upon. When a reader begins to relate to a story in terms of his or her own life, the story simply makes more sense. We know ourselves better than we know anything else, so to read a book through the eyes of our own lives is the essence of "creating meaning." The notion that we bring ourselves into the books we read, that we weave our life stories into the stories that we read, is a deep truth. To teach children to learn to make sense of a text for themselves is teaching them not *what* to think, but *how* to think. When we teach children to connect, we are teaching them to pay attention to moments, feelings, characters, and places in a story that trigger links to their own feelings, characters, and places in their life story. Reading unlocks the memories that are the backdrop of our lives.

After a Reading Power workshop, a teacher came up to me to thank me for helping her solve one of the greatest mysteries of her life: why she has never liked borrowing books from the library. She explained that she had always been an avid reader, that reading books had been a hobby of hers all her life. She had, she was sometimes ashamed to admit, spent a small fortune on books. Friends and colleagues always wondered why she didn't just go to the library to borrow books to read instead of buying so many. But she had never, she told me, enjoyed borrowing books from the library. She had tried, but preferred instead to buy them. She never knew the reason for this, she said, until she heard me talk about connecting. She realized that, when she reads a book, the book becomes "her story" and that after experiencing the power of connecting through reading it, returning it to the library meant sharing her life with the next person who might come along and borrow that book. An extreme example perhaps, but one that clearly illustrates the power of connecting.

> **When readers connect…**
>
> - the story reminds them of people, places, and feelings they have experienced.
> - their minds become filled with memories.
> - they are making sense of the text in terms of their own experiences and background knowledge.
> - they can make connections to pictures, events, characters, and feelings from the story.
> - they are most likely reading books about realistic situations, such as family, feelings, friendship, school, siblings, pets, vacations, etc.

Our life experiences deepen and enrich our life story to create the well of experiences from which we draw when we read. Unfortunately, not all children come to us with a wealth of life stories upon which to draw. We need to be aware of this and to try to provide stories they will be able to connect with successfully: stories about school, family, friendship, siblings, losing a tooth, birthday parties, and pets. We need to be constantly modeling our own connections and allowing children to share theirs. Just as we do not connect to every book we read, we

Your life is a story, it's just not written down on paper.

"A writer only begins a book. A reader finishes it."
—Samuel Johnson

cannot expect our students to connect to every book. If a child does not connect to a story one day, it's okay. Encourage the child to connect to the next story. We can gently nudge children in the direction we want them to go by continually modeling our thinking and encouraging them to become more confident in their connections. Viviane, a Grade 2 student at Laura Secord, was a keen Connecter. During the Group Connect lessons (see page 49), she was one of the first to put her sticky note in the book. But after reading the story *Franklin's New Friend* to the class, Viviane was the only student who still had her sticky in her hand. When I questioned why she hadn't added her sticky to the book, she responded, "How can I make a connection to that book? I am NOT a turtle!"

New Thinking about Connecting

Going Deeper with Connections

"If books could have more, give more, be more, show more, they would still need readers, who bring to them sound and smell and light and all the rest that can't be in books. The book needs you."
—Gary Paulson, *The Winter Room*

Connecting is one of the easiest strategies for children to grasp. We need to be careful, however, that we are guiding students to make connections that are meaningful. While it might be easy to look at a picture of a dog and say, "My uncle has a dog," that is not elevating a students' thinking or understanding. It is up to us to guide our students towards making connections that are going to move them forward in their thinking. In my years of teaching students how to make connections to text, I have witnessed students making connections to just about everything. And while we can celebrate that our students are engaged and participating, those of us who have experienced these random connections will know that not all of them enhance understanding, and they can quickly derail a lesson! It is essential, therefore, when teaching students how to make connections, to explain and model this important point. You will find lessons on *going deeper* on page 50.

Anyone who has taught students how to make connections has experienced a student going off topic, sharing a connection that has nothing to do with the story and stimulating a chain reaction in which the rest of the students make "connections" that have less and less to do with what is being read. While I struggled when this happened more frequently than I liked, I realized that I was partly to blame for it happening: I was so focused on the strategy that I, too, had lost sight of the content of the story. I developed the BIBB (Bring It Back to the Book) (see lesson on page 51) to address this problem and to help both students and teacher refocus on the content.

Brain Pockets

Another concept that evolved to address connections that stray from the reading content is the use of Brain Pockets. See lesson on page 46 for using my visual for teaching students about their schema. The idea for the Brain Pockets started from working with a student I had several years ago. He was a bright boy, but when he raised his hand, I tended to avoid eye contact! No matter what we were reading or talking about in class, his thinking often took him far away from the text. It was frustrating—I didn't want to discourage him from using his imagination, but making connections to aliens kidnapping grandmothers from Halifax was not exactly the kind of connection I was looking for when we were reading a book about Canada. With brain pockets, I was able to tell him that he was "in the wrong pocket" rather than telling him his connection was wrong.

Sequential Lessons for Connecting

Lesson 1 (Teacher Directed): Introducing the Power to Connect, Part 1

- Remind students that good readers are also good thinkers. Using the Reading Power Model, place the Connect piece inside the head. Explain that connecting is one way a reader can think about a story, and that today you will be talking about what connecting is.
- Ask students to make a circle with their finger and thumb on each hand.
- At the count of 3, students are to connect their circles. Tell them that there are different ways and to consider different possibilities. Do not explain any further than that.
- Once students have connected their circles, invite them to share and compare their connection with others.
- Notice and reflect on the different ways student connected their circles (Linking circles, touching side by side, circles on top of each other, making funny upside-down glasses over their eyes).
- Explain that everyone was connecting circles but did it in different ways.
- Ask students for other words that might mean the same as connecting (linking, merging, joining, putting together).
- Explain that, when readers connect, they are merging or joining together the book with their thinking. Show that the book is one circle and the reading brain is the other circle.
- Ask students what is inside their brain that they might be connecting to (memories, experiences, people, feelings, places).
- Draw a brain on the board or interactive whiteboard. Explain that the brain is a powerful part of our body because it is the control centre for everything, including our thinking.
- Explain that the brain is also an amazing place because it is the storage place for our thinking. Everything we think about and learn about gets stored inside the small space that is our brain.
- Explain the word *schema*, which I refer to as our "thinking storage." Another way of describing schema is like a computer storage filled with files of different information.

> I like to think of my brain as a storage place for my thinking. Inside this huge storage place of thinking, we have different places to store our thinking. I call these Brain Pockets. We have three main pockets in our brains: experiences and memories of those experiences are stored in the Memory Pocket; information and facts we learn are stored in the Fact Pocket; and creative thinking is stored in the Imagination Pocket.

(As you talk, divide the drawn brain into three sections and label them.)

When discussing where connections come from, remind students that connections can be stored in our hearts, as well as in our brains. Connections tied to feelings and emotions, in fact, are often the most power and meaningful.

When talking to students about what is stored our Memory Pocket, I like to refer to the collection of experiences and memories as chapters in my life story. A person's life is a story and every experience we have in our life adds another chapter to it. It's amazing to think that the memories of our life are stored in a tiny pocket of our brain!

- Explain that these brain pockets are very important when we read because they help us with our understanding. Depending on the type of book being read, the reader will find connections in different pockets. Refer to visual above.
- Give examples: connections to a story about friends come from the Memory Pocket; connections to reading about volcanoes come from a Fact Pocket; connections when reading Harry Potter come from the Imagination Pocket.
- Optional: Provide students with a brain graphic with blank pockets and invite them to draw or write in each section to illustrate important memories, facts they know a lot about, and things they imagine they might be connecting to.
- End the lesson:

I also use Brain Pockets when I teach writing, as an illustration of ideas for writing and where writers get them.

Beatrice Doesn't Want To by Laura Numeroff and *Matchbox Diary* by Sid Fleischman are books I like to share at the end of this lesson. Both are excellent illustrations of making connections and the use of Memory Pockets.

> For the next few weeks, we will be learning and practicing how to make connections when we read.

Students can write or draw a reflection about what they learned about Making Connections in their Reading Power notebook.

Lesson 2 (Teacher Directed): Introducing the Power to Connect, Part 2

It is important to make children aware of the individuality that comes from making sense of text through our connections. There is no one right connection, because we use our own schema or Brain Pockets to construct meaning.

- Remind students that they are learning about how readers can understand what they read by making connections. Review the idea of Brain Pockets with them.

The book *Rondo in C* by Paul Fleischman is a brilliant example of making connections to music. It is out of print, but if you are able to find a copy in your local library or through a used book site, I highly recommend it.

- Read *Rondo in C* by Paul Fleischman or *Once Upon an Ordinary School Day* by Colin McNaughton if you are able to get copies.
- After reading one of those books, ask students: "Why is it that everyone in the room is listening to the same piece of music (or reading the same story) but they are all thinking of different things? Why isn't everyone making connections to the same thing?" (Because we are all different and our Brain Pockets are filled with different memories, experiences, and knowledge)

Another option for this lesson is to have the students fold their paper in half, with each side of the paper representing one of their brain pockets. The first time they listen to the music, they draw their Memory connections on one half of the sheet; the second time, they draw their Imagination connections on the other half.

"Books are mirrors: you only see in them what you already have inside you."
—Carlos Ruiz Zafón, *The Shadow of the Wind*

- Explain that there is no one right way to connect, and that two people can read the same book but make different connections. Tell students that what triggers a memory for one person might not trigger a memory for anybody else. Or two people might make a connection to the same part of the story for completely different reasons.
- Give everyone a blank piece of paper. Explain that you are going to be playing a piece of music and they will practice making connections.
- Play a piece of music and invite students to close their eyes and listen; I like to use Vivaldi's "Spring" from *The Four Seasons* or *The Flight of the Bumblebee* by Rimsky-Korsakov. While they listen, students are to think about what the music reminds them of or makes them think about.
- Invite students to draw a picture of the connection they made with the music. When everyone is finished, invite students to share their connection with a partner.
- Display the papers around the room and discuss how everyone listened to the same piece of music but made different connections.
- End the lesson by generating a Making Connections anchor chart to post in the classroom.

SAMPLE CONNECT ANCHOR CHART

Good Readers Make Connections!

We make connections to…
- Our memories, experiences, and feelings
- Facts and information we already know
- Our imagination
- Other books, movies, or TV shows

This reminds me of…
This makes make me think about…
I'm making a connection to the part when…

Lessons 3–4 (Teacher Directed): Modeling Your Thinking

I discovered that it is possible to buy sticky notes in the shape of a thinking bubble! This is a wonderful too to use when modeling your thinking.

- Find your special Connect Book; i.e., a picture book that elicits strong connections and memories for you.
- Model a read-aloud/think-aloud with this special Connect book, using sticky notes to mark your connections with a *C* or a Thinking Bubble to hold up when you share your connection. Pause on a page, insert your sticky note or hold up your Thinking Bubble, and model, using this language: "This part of the story reminds me of…"
- Students wishing to participate while you are modeling can do so with a "quiet connections thumbs-up" (see page 39).
- Follow with at least two more similar lessons, using different books, within a few days. As you model, try to make sure that you are connecting to each of these: an event from the story, a character, and a feeling.

Finding Your Special Connect Book

My special Connect book, the one I always use to model that first Connect lesson, is Robert McKlosky's *One Morning in Maine* because it reminds me of summer holidays spent with my family on Mayne Island. The story is filled with so many fond memories of my childhood, it feels as if it was written about me. One teacher who was born in Saskatchewan uses *If You're Not From the Prairie* by Henry Ripplinger. It takes her two days to read because each page is a story from her childhood on the farm. Jodi Carson, a Literacy Mentor, searched for weeks until she finally found her Connect book: *Tales of a Gambling Grandma* by David Kaur Khalsa, because it reminds her of when her grandmother used to teach her and her sister how to play blackjack every Friday night. It may take you a few visits to the library to find your own special Connect book. The students might not remember the story you read, but they certainly will remember your connections to it!

Lesson 5 (Guided Group Practice): Group Connect

Some primary teachers find sticky notes too distracting for their students and choose, instead, to give each student a Thinking Bubble. Thinking Bubbles can be made by cutting out a bubble shape and gluing it on a craft stick. Students hold up their Thinking Bubbles during the read aloud; once they have shared, the bubble is collected. The goal is that every student will have a chance to share a connection before the end of the story.

- Explain to students that they will be participating in a read-aloud by paying attention to their thinking and by noticing when they make connections in the story.
- Pass out one sticky note to each student. Ask students to put their name and a big letter *C* on it.
- Read aloud a book from the Connect bin and have students listen for all their connections.
- Read the book again, and have each student come up and put his/her sticky note on the page where his/her best connection was made, or where the student's thinking voice "was the loudest." Students are not sharing at this point, simply placing their sticky notes in the book when you get to the right page.
- Continue to model by placing your own sticky note on one of the pages.
- Model how you want students to share: "I put my sticky on the page where…. This reminded me of…"
- Invite students to share their connections out loud with a partner. When partners are sharing, circulate around the room, listening for all connections. Choose one pair of students to come up to the front to model their connections. Choose the pair who really went beyond a simple statement like "This reminds me of my brother" to sharing a "chapter" of their life stories.
- Depending on time, students can chose one of the Connect templates (see pages 58–62) to write and/or draw their connections.
- Suggested books for this lesson: *Some Things Are Scary* by Florence Parry Heide; *Courage* by Bernard Waber; *The Party* by Barbara Reid; *One of Those Days, The OKAY Book,* or *It's Not Fair!* by Amy Krouse Rosenthal; *No, David!* by David Shannon; *My Brave Book of Firsts* by Jamie Lee Curtis; *Twelve Terrible Things* by Marty Kelley.
- You can follow this lesson with similar Group Connects and invite students to turn and share their connections with a partner. Choose one or two students to share their connections with the class. This informal sharing is an opportunity to monitor students' connections and to give praise for the strong connections, guidance for the weaker ones, and encouragement for the non-connectors.
- You might choose to have students draw and/or write about their connections: choose template Making Connections #1 or #2 on pages 61 and 62.

Lessons 6–7 (Guided Group Practice): Expanding Connections

- Create a large chart (Expanding Your Connections #1 on page 58) to display in the classroom.
- Explain to students that when we read, we can connect to different parts of the book: part of the story, a picture, a character, or a feeling.
- Repeat Group Connect lesson (page 49). After students have placed their stickies in the book, explain that you will be returning their stickies shortly. Refer to the chart and tell them you would like the stickies placed on the column where they think they made their connection today. Model with your sticky note and explain your thinking.
- Page by page, pass the stickies back and have students put them on the chart.
- The next day, remind students where they put their stickies on the chart. Encourage them to try to put their stickies in a different spot today during the Group Connect.
- This same lesson can used when introducing students to different ways we make connections. Depending on the grade level, you can introduce students to T–S (Text-to-Self: *This book reminds me of the time when I…*), T–T (Text-to-Text: *This book reminds me of another book I've read*), and T–W (Text to World: *This book reminds me of something I already know about the world*) connections. (See template on page 59.)
- In conjunction with the Brain Pockets lesson (page 46), you can also invite students to make T–M (Text-to-Memory), T–F (Text-to-Fact), and T–I (Text-to-Imagination) connections. (See Brain Pockets template on page 63.)

Lesson 8–9 (Teacher Directed): Going Deeper with Connections: Quick and Deep-Thinking

Most students learn to connect relatively easily, but there is a tendency for some to connect to everything. While it can be initially exciting to hear them making connections, not all connections enhance understanding. Helping students to make effective, meaningful connections is an important next step.

- Explain that not all connections help readers understand the story better.
- Introduce the idea of Quick connections (e.g., "I have a blue hat like the one in that picture.") and Deep-Thinking connections (e.g., "That reminds me of the time when I got teased at school for wearing dresses every day and I felt really embarrassed.").
- Spend time modeling the difference between the two levels of connections, so that students can begin to see and understand the difference.
- Sometimes I invite students to listen to my connections and, if they think my connection is a Quick one, they can snap their fingers. If they think the connection is a Deep-Thinking one, they can point to their heads.

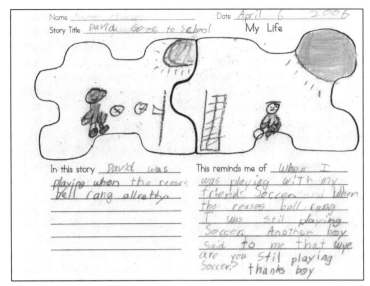

Name _____   Date _April 6 2006_

Story Title _David Goes to School_   My Life

In this story _David was playing when the reases bell rang allretty._

This reminds me of _When I was playing with my friends' Soccer and when the reases bell rang I was stil playing Soccer. Another boy said to me that are you stil playing Soccer? thanks boy_

Grade 2 Sample

Lesson 10–11 (Guided Group Practice): Going Deeper with Connections: Put On Your BIBB!

I refer to these connections as "burnt hamburger connections," because I once had a student make a connection to their dad's burnt barbecue hamburgers after seeing a picture of a hamburger in the book. The book was about a boy who dumps his best friend to hang out with the new cool kid—not about cooking hamburgers!

Students sometimes get side-tracked by a story they want to share that has nothing to do with the story you are reading. This can cause a chain reaction—soon many students are making connections to the first student's story and not the book. Within a short time, the book is off the radar entirely! The more often we can guide students to make relevant, meaningful connections—as opposed to quick, random, or off-track connections—the more likely they will learn to find meaningful connections.

- Explain to students that not all connections are going to help them find meaning.
- When a student does go off track with his/her thinking, guide them to bring their thinking back to the book.
- Explain the acronym BIBB stands for Bring It Back to the Book, with "It" referring to their thinking.

A small plastic baby bib with *BIBB* on it hangs in my classroom. Whenever a student makes a connection that is not connected to the story, I will stop that student and say, "I think you need to put on your BIBB." (I no longer actually tie it on them!)

- When a student makes a connection that is not connected to the story, remind that student of BIBB.
- Ask: *What is this story about?* and *Has your connection helped you to understand the story better?*

Lessons 12–13 (Independent Practice): Trading Connections

These sticky notes act as small windows into your students' thinking and can be used for assessment.

- Have each student choose his or own book from the Connect collection (see book list on pages 55–57). Provide each with their own sticky notes.
- Ask them to read silently and mark their connections with their sticky notes. Older students can jot down notes about their connections on each sticky; younger students will simply code the sticky with a *C* and their names.
- As students finish, they can find a partner and share their connections. Encourage students to find a page where they both had stickies on the same page. These double-connection pages can be shared with the class.
- This lesson works very well if, after students mark their connections, they trade books with a partner and mark their connections using different-colored

sticky notes. Partners then get together to share and compare their connections from both books.

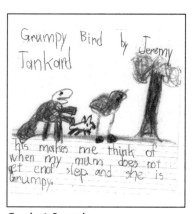

Grade 1 Sample

Lessons 14–16 (Independent Practice): Expanding Connections Through Writing

- Explain how each sticky note placed in a book represents a little chapter of a student's life.
- Model how to expand this into writing by choosing one of your previous connections and writing it out—with details, names, and feelings—on chart paper.
- Invite students to choose their own book to read (from the collection of Connect books, if possible) and to use sticky notes to mark connections they make while they read. (I usually limit sticky notes to 3–5 each.)
- After students read and mark their connections independently, have them choose the connection where their "thinking voice was the loudest" and expand this connection into writing. This could be done by writing about it in a journal, or using one of the templates (pages 58–62).
- Many teachers give students Reading Power Notebooks or duotangs for these writing extensions. Students can peel the stickies from the book they read, stick them on one page of the notebook with title and author at the top, then choose one of the connections to write about. I like to have a variety of different templates for the students to chose from. You will find examples of these on pages 58–62.
- Rule: Never put a book back into the book bin and "leave your thinking behind." Sticky notes must be peeled off before a book is returned. Students can use the Independent Connections organizer on page 66 to keep their sticky notes.

Lesson 17 (Independent Practice): Finding Your Own Connect Book

- Review the concept of the Connect power.
- Older students can be given the assignment of finding their own special Connect book in the school or public library.
  - Go to the library and search for your special Connect book.
  - Write about the picture book that you made strong connections with:
    1. Give a brief summary of the story
    2. Use examples that show how you connected to the book through the events, pictures, characters, or feelings.
    3. Explain whether you made T–S, T–T, T–W connections. Give examples.
    4. Explain what makes this book special to you.
  - Prepare an oral presentation for the class on your Connect book.
- Books can be displayed, along with the written connections and photo of the student.
- As teacher, you can participate in the display with your own Connect book.

Some teachers who are implementing Reading Power begin their first staff meeting in the fall by sharing their personal Connect books with each other. It's a wonderful way to get to know your colleagues!

My Connect Book

Title: The Hockey Sweater

Author: Roch Carrier

Illustrator: Sheldon Cohen

The book I chose to be my special Connect book is *The Hockey Sweater* by Roch Carrier. It is the story of a boy who lives in a small town in Montreal. All the kids in the small town are crazy about hockey and they play hockey and think about hockey all day long. Their favorite team is the Montreal Canadiens and their favorite player is Maurice Richard. The boy ends up getting a new hockey jersey, but by mistake, it is a Toronto Maple Leafs jersey and not a Montreal Canadiens jersey. His mum makes him wear it anyways and his friends and the coach won't let him play.

I made a lot of connections to events, characters and feelings from this book. The main character really reminded me of my younger brother, Pete. Pete loved hockey and loved the Montreal Canadiens more than anything else. He, like the main character, would have been devastated if he had to wear a Toronto jersey. I also made connections to the events. The story showed how important hockey was to this town. Everybody was involved in hockey whether they were playing or listening to the game on the radio. This reminds me of growing up in the small town of Trail, BC, where everyone lived and loved hockey. I made connections to the feelings in the book. It reminded me of the intense feeling my brother showed when the Montreal Canadiens lost. When the main character broke his stick in frustration, it reminded me of my brother hitting the television when his favorite team lost—especially to the Toronto Maple Leafs.

This book reminded me of things in my own childhood and also it reminded me how a town or country can go crazy when their hockey team is winning or in the playoffs. I know how the boy in the story must have felt because I also felt that way.

This book is my special Connect book because when I read it, it made me feel like I was reading about my own brother and my own town.

Lesson 18: Reflective Journal

Have students record their thoughts about this new strategy and what they've learned about connecting. *How has connecting while you read helped you to understand the story better? Show me or tell me about your thinking.*

Extended Connect Lessons

- Introduce students to different connect codes: T–S (Text-to-Self), T–T (Text- to-Text), T–W (Text-to-World). See Expanding Your Connections #2 on page 59.
- Have older students read a Connect book to their buddies and share connections.
- Invite students make connections when reading library books or books during independent reading.
- Have students and parents mark connections together in the same book when doing home reading or during student-led conferences. (See Connect home reading sheet on page 175)

For Connect texts to use with older students, see page 57.

Connecting for Older Students

After introducing, modeling, and practicing the strategy of connecting, use the concept to teach students different points of view: e.g., objective and omniscient. Read excerpts from Connect stories to model examples:

> Objective narration: difficult to make connections to because the reader has to infer all of the characters' feelings

> Omniscient narration: easiest to connect to because the reader has more personal thoughts and feelings to base those connections on

Writing Extensions

- Okay Connection: Read *The Okay Book* by Amy Krouse Rosenthal and invite students to draw or write about something they are just "okay" at. Use I'm Okay! template on page 65.
- ME connections: Read *I Like Me!* by Nancy Carlson and invite students to write about themselves: you can use the Connecting to Me! template on page 64.
- Color Connections: Read *My Blue is Happy* by Jessica Young and invite students to choose a color and make a connection to it.
- Toy Connections: Read *Too Many Toys!* by David Shannon and invite students to draw or write about a toy they would want to keep, and about a toy they could give away.
- Pajama Connections: Read *The Cat's Pajamas* by Catherine Foreman and invite students to draw and/or write about their own pajamas.
- Making Mistakes Connections: Read *It's OKAY to Make Mistakes* by Todd Parr and invite students to write and/or draw about a mistake they have made.

Assessing Connections

While it can be challenging to assess thinking, we can certainly differentiate between a connection that enhances understanding and one that doesn't. This rubric can help you provide feedback to students and parents, and will give you information on which of your students might need more support in the *going deeper* lessons.

The OK Book

I'm OK at...
Skating. Sometimes
When I need to Start
I fall down and when I
want to get back up
the ice is so slipery I
fall back down.

Grade 2 Sample

NY = Not Yet Meeting Grade Level Expectations
M = Meeting Expectations at a Minimal Level
FM = Fully Meeting Grade Expectations
EX = Exceeding Expectations

ASSESSMENT RUBRIC FOR CONNECTIONS

Making Connections	NY	M	FM	EX
Generates connections independently while reading with little or no support.				
Demonstrates an understanding of the difference between "quick" and "deep-thinking" connections.				
Makes connections that enhance understanding and are directly related to the meaning of the text.				
Is able to explain how his/her connection has helped them understand the text better (BIBB).				

Connect Books

Choose from the following books to create a collection of Connect books for your classroom or library. Set aside a few Gems to use for your modeling lessons. Try to include a few books from each category to unsure a variety of connect topics.

BOOKS ON THE CONCEPT OF CONNECTING

Fleischman, Paul. *Rondo In C* (P, I)

Fleischman, Paul. *Matchbox Diary*

Macdonald, Anne Marie. *The Memory Stone* (P, I)

McNaughton, Colin. *Once Upon an Ordinary School Day* (P, I)

Numeroff, Laura. *Beatrice Doesn't Want To!* (P)

BOOKS ABOUT FAMILY/SIBLINGS

Blume, Judy. *The Pain and the Great One* (I)

Browne, Anthony. *My Dad* (P, I)

Browne, Anthony. *My Mum* (P, I)

Castillo, Lauren. *Nana in the City* (P)

Cooper, Elisha. *Homer* (P, I)

Fergus, Maureen. *InvisiBill* (P, I)

Gliori, Debi. *My Little Brother* (P, I)

Hoberman, Mary Ann. *All Kinds of Families* (P, I)

Hoffman, Mary. *The Great Big Book of Families* (P)

Hughes, Shirley. *The Trouble with Jack.* (P, I)

Khan, Rukhsana. *Big Red Lollipop* (P, I)

Kopelke, Lisa. *The Younger Brother's Survival Guide* (I)

Lang, Suzanne. *Families, Families, Families!* (P)

Light, Kelly. *Louise Loves Art* (P)

Juster, Norton. *The Hello, Goodbye Window* (P, I)

McPhail, David. *Sisters* (P)

Parr, Todd. *The Family Book* (P)

Parr, Todd. *We Belong Together: A Book About Adoption and Families* (P)

Petricic, Dusan. *My Family Tree and Me* (P, I)

Polacco, Patricia. *My Rotten Red-Headed Older Brother* (I)

Reid, Barbara. *The Party* (P, I)

Rosenthal, Amy Krouse. *Little Miss, Big Sis* (P)

Rylant, Cynthia. *The Relatives Came* (I)

Urban, Linda. *Little Red Henry* (P)

BOOKS ABOUT FEELINGS

Aliki. *Feelings* (P)

Anholt, Catherine & Laurence. *Good Days, Bad Days* (P)

Anholt, Catherine & Laurence. *What Makes Me Happy* (P)

Arnaldo, Monica. *The Little Book of Big Fears* (P)

Bang, Molly. *When Sophie Gets Angry* (P, I)

Blumenthal, Diana Cain. *I'm Not Invited?* (P, I)

Browne, Anthony. *What If?* (I)

Cain, Janan. *The Way I Feel* (P, I)

Cain, Janan. *The Way I Act* (P, I)

Churchill, Vicki. *Sometimes I Like to Curl Up in a Ball* (P)

Curtis, Jamie Lee. *Today I Feel Silly* (P)

Daly, Cathleen. *Emily's Blue Period* (P, I)

Fernandes, Eugenie. *A Difficult Day* (P)

Henkes, Kevin. *Wemberly Worried* (P, I)

Hoffman, Mary. *The Great Big Book of Feelings* (P)

Heide, Florence Parry. *Some Things Are Scary* (P, I)

Kelley, Marty. *Twelve Terrible Things* (I)

Nemiroff, Marc. *Shy Spaghetti and Excited Eggs: A Kid's Menu of Feelings* (P)

Negley, Keith. *Tough Guys Have Feelings Too* (P, I)

Parr, Todd. *The Feelings Book* (P)

Rosenthal, Amy Krouse. *One of Those Days* (I)

Seeger, Laura Vaccarro. *I Used To Be Afraid* (P)

Spires, Ashley. *The Most Magnificent Thing* (P, I)

Van Hout, Miles. *Happy* (P, I)

Willems, Mo. *My Friend is Sad* (P)

Willems, Mo. *The Pigeon Has Feelings Too!* (P)

Witek, Jo. *In My Heart: A Book of Feelings* (P)

Waber, Bernard. *Courage* (P, I)

Young, Jessica. *My Blue is Happy* (P, I)

BOOKS ABOUT FRIENDSHIP

Bourgeois, Paulette. *Franklin's Secret Club* (P)

Brown, Peter. *You Will Be My Friend* (P)

Carlson, Nancy. *My Best Friend Moved Away* (P)

Dunklee, Annika. *ME, Too!* (P)

Fergus, Maureen. *Buddy and Earl* (P)

Ferry, Beth. *Stick and Stone* (P, I)

Fitzpatrick, Marie Louise. *The New Kid* (P)

Freedman, Deborah. *The Story of Fish & Snail* (P)

Freedman, Deborah. *By Mouse & Frog* (P)

Gavin, Ciara. *Room for Bear* (P)

Henkes, Kevin. *Chester's Way* (P, I)

Hills, Tad. *Duck and Goose* (P)

Juster, Norton. *Neville* (I)
McBratney, Sam. *I'm Sorry* (SR) (P)
Oldland, Nicholas. *Walk on the Wild Side* (P, I)
O'Neill, Alexis. *The Worst Best Friend* (P, I)
Polacco, Patricia. *Bully* (I)
Rodman, Mary Ann. *My Best Friend* (P, I)
Rosenthal, Amy Krouse. *Friendshape* (P)
Santat, Dan. *The Adventures of Beekle: The Unimaginary Friend* (P, I)
Shea, Bob. *Ballet Cat: The Totally Secret Secret* (P)
Steig, William. *Amos and Boris* (I)
Van Hout, Mies *Friends* (P, I)
Watt, Mélanie. *Scaredy Squirrel Makes a Friend* (P, I)

BOOKS ABOUT SCHOOL

Ahlberg, Allan. *Starting School* (P)
Ashley, Bernard. *Cleversticks* (P)
Brown, Marc. *Monkey: Not Ready For Kindergarten* (P)
Cox, Phil Roxbee. *Don't Be a Bully, Billy* (P, I)
Fraser, Mary Ann. *I.Q. Goes to School* (P, I)
Friedman, Laurie. *Back-to-School Rules* (P, I)
Gaiman, Neil. *Chu's First Day of School* (P)
Henkes, Kevin. *Lily's Purple Plastic Purse* (P, I)
Lefebvre, Jason. *Too Much Glue* (P, I)
Lester, Helen. *Me First* (P)
Lorenz, Albert. *The Exceptionally, Extraordinarily Ordinary First Day of School* (P, I)
Mackintosh, David. *Marshall Armstrong Is New to Our School* (P, I)
Mann, Jennifer K. *I Will Never Get a Star on Mrs. Benson's Blackboard* (P, I)
McNamara, Margaret. *The Playground Problem* (P)
O'Neill, Alexis. *The Recess Queen* (P, I)
Rapp, Jennifer. *I Can Wait for the Bell to Ring* (I)
Rathmann, Peggy. *Ruby the Copycat* (P, I)
Rosenberry, Vera. *Vera's First Day of School* (P)
Schwartz, Amy. *Things I Learned in Second Grade* (P)
Shannon, David. *David Goes To School* (P, I)
Simms, Laura. *Rotten Teeth.* (P, I)
Torrey, Richard. *Ally-Saurus & the First Day of School* (P)
Vernick, Audrey. *First Grade Dropout* (P)
Viorst, Judith. *And Two Boys Booed* (P)
Wells, Rosemary. *Timothy Goes to School* (P, I)
Winters, Kay. *This School Year Will Be the BEST!* (P)

BOOKS ABOUT GRIEF AND HEALING

Aliki. *The Two of Them.* (P, I)
Bagley, Jessica. *Boats for Papa* (P)
Bunting, Eve. *The Memory String* (P, I)

DePaola, Tomie. *Nana Upstairs and Nana Downstairs.* (I)
Durant, Alan. *Always and Forever.* (P)
Jeffers, Oliver. *The Heart and the Bottle* (P, I)
Lunde, Stein Erik. *My Father's Arms Are a Boat* (I)
Moundlic, Charlotte. *The Scar* (P, I)
Rosen, Michael. *Michael Rosen's Sad Book* (I)
Teckentrup, Britta. *The Memory Tree* (P, I)
Varley, Susan. *Badger's Parting Gifts.* (P)
Viorst, Judith. *The Tenth Good Thing about Barney.* (P, I)
Wilhelm, Hans. *I'll Always Love You* (P, I)
Willems, Mo. *City Dog, Country Frog* (P, I)

MEMOIRS

Curtis, Jamie Lee. *When I Was Little: A Four Year Old's Memoir of Her Youth* (P, I)
Curtis. Jamie Lee. *My Brave Book of Firsts* (P, I)
McLaughlin, Patricia. *What You Know First* (P, I)
McLaughlin, Patricia. *You Were the First* (P, I)
O'Leary, Sara. *When I Was Small* (P, I)
O'Leary, Sara. *When You Were Small* (P, I)
Rylant, Cynthia. *Birthday Presents.* (P, I)

SELF-IDENTITY, SELF-EXPRESSION

Browne, Anthony. *Things I Like* (P)
Carlson, Nancy. *I Like Me!* (P)
Chodos-Irvine, Margaret. *Ella Sarah Gets Dressed* (P)
Curtis, Jamie Lee. *I'm Gonna Like Me: Letting Off a Little Self-Esteem* (P)
DePaola, Tomie. *Oliver Button Is a Sissy* (P, I)
Gillmor, Don. *When Vegetables Go Bad* (P, I)
Hale, Bruce. *Clark the Shark* (P)
Hall, Michael. *Red: A Crayon's Story* (P, I)
Heap, Sue. *Red Rockets and Rainbow Jelly* (P)
Offill, Jenny. *17 Things I'm Not Allowed to Do Anymore* (P, I)
Parr, Todd. *It's Okay to Be Different* (P)
Petty, Dave. *I Don't Want to Be a Frog* (P, I)
Shannon, David. *David Gets in Trouble.* (P, I)
Shannon, David. *No, David!* (P, I)
Stinson, Kathy. *Red is Best.* (P)
Young, Jessica. *My Blue is Happy* (P, I)
Zolotow, Charlotte. *William's Doll.* (P, I)

BOOKS WITH ABORIGINAL THEMES

Bruchac, Joseph. *The First Strawberries* (P)
Einarson, Earl. *The Moccasins* (P)
Gear, Alison. *Taan's Moons* (P)
Highway, Tomson. *Fox On the Ice: Maageesees Maskwameek Kaapit* (P, I)
Kalluk, Celina. *Sweetest Kulu* (P)

McCain, Becky Ray. *Grandmother's Dreamcatcher* (P, I)

McLeod, Elaine. *Lessons from Mother Earth* (P)

Olsen, Sylvia. *Yetsa's Sweater* (P, I)

Sellars, Willie. *Dipnetting with Dad* (P, I)

Smith, Cynthia Leitich. *Jingle Dancer* (P)

Spalding, Andrea. *Solomon's Tree* (P, I)

Suzuki, David. *Salmon Forest* (P, I)

Teachers and Students of SD 50. *B is for Basketball* (P, I)

Waterton, Betty. *A Salmon for Simon* (P, I)

CONNECT TEXTS FOR OLDER STUDENTS (GRADES 8–12)

Angelou, Maya. "Still I Rise" (poem)

Bruce, Michael. "Gentlemen, Your Verdict" (short story)

Collins, Billy. "Another Reason Why I Don't Keep a Gun in the House" (poem)

Ellis, Sarah. "Catch" (short story)

Hill, Susan. "The Badness Within Him" (short story)

Kelley, Marty. *Twelve Terrible Things* (picture book)

Koyczan, Shane. "To This Day" (poem)

Matheson, Richard. "Button, Button" (short story)

Shakespeare, William. *Romeo and Juliet; A Midsummer Night's Dream*

Storm, Jennifer. *Deadly Loyalties* (* strong content)

Tan, Shaun. *The Red Tree* (picture book)

Valgardson, W.D. "Saturday Climbing" (short story)

Expanding Your Connections #1

Name: _____   Date: _____

Connecting to...

the story	a picture	a character	a feeling

Expanding Your Connections #2

Name: _____   Date: _____

Text to Self (T-S) . . . to ourselves	Text to Text (T-T) . . . to other books	Text to World (T-W) . . . to the world

Pembroke Publishers © 2015 *Reading Power, Revised and Expanded* by Adrienne Gear ISBN 978-1-55138-310-1

Connecting Stories

Name: _____   Date: _____

Story Title: _____

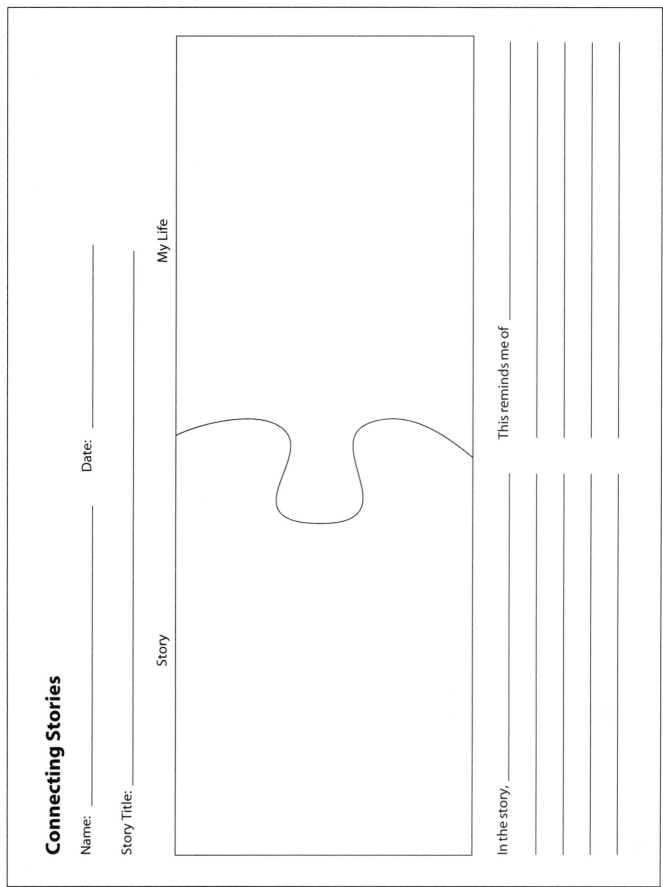

Story

My Life

In the story, _____

This reminds me of _____

Pembroke Publishers © 2015 *Reading Power, Revised and Expanded* by Adrienne Gear ISBN 978-1-55138-310-1

Making Connections #1

Name: _____ Date: _____

[ ]

Title: _____ Author: _____

This part of the story reminds me of . . . .

_____

_____

_____

_____

Pembroke Publishers © 2015 *Reading Power, Revised and Expanded* by Adrienne Gear ISBN 978-1-55138-310-1

Making Connections #2

Name: _____   Date: _____

Title: _____   Author: _____

In the story...	This reminds me of...
_____ _____ _____ _____ _____	_____ _____ _____ _____ _____
_____ _____ _____ _____ _____	_____ _____ _____ _____ _____
_____ _____ _____ _____	_____ _____ _____ _____

Pembroke Publishers © 2015 *Reading Power, Revised and Expanded* by Adrienne Gear ISBN 978-1-55138-310-1

Brain Pockets

Name: _____   Date: _____

Fact Pocket

Imagination Pocket

Memory Pocket

Our brains are the storage place for thinking. Thinking is organized into three places in our brains called Brain Pockets. Memories and experiences are stored in our MEMORY Pocket; information and knowledge is stored in our FACT Pocket; and our creative thinking is stored in our IMAGINATION Pocket. Depending on what we are reading, we can go to different pockets to find our connections.

Memory Pocket Connection	Fact Pocket Connection	Imagination Connection

Connecting to Me!

Name: _____

Date: _____

I like _____	My friend is _____
I like to go to the _____	My favorite animal is _____

I'm Okay!

Name: _____   Date: _____

I'm OKAY at…

_____

_____

_____

_____

_____

_____

_____

_____

_____

Pembroke Publishers © 2015 *Reading Power, Revised and Expanded* by Adrienne Gear ISBN 978-1-55138-310-1

Independent Connections

Name: _____   Date: _____

Title: _____

Author: _____

Sticky Notes:

- -

Name: _____   Date: _____

Title: _____

Author: _____

Sticky Notes:

4 The Power to Visualize

Visualize Chant
(snap or clap the beat)

You don't use your eyes when you visualize
You don't use your eyes when you visualize
You don't use your eyes when you visualize
You use your BRAIN! (add jazz hands)

Visualize Song
Diane Martin, Spul'u'kwuks School
(to the tune of "Twinkle Twinkle Little Star")

When my teacher reads a book
Then my brain begins to look,
Seeing pictures in my head
As the story's being read.
Making pictures, me and you,
You can THINK some pictures too!

✳ ✳ ✳

"When your head is full of pictures, they just have to come out."
—Bill Maynard, *Incredible Ned*

During a long car ride, an eight-year-old boy passes the time listening to a tape recording of *The Hatchet* by Gary Paulson. For nearly three hours, he does not speak and is completely absorbed in the story. Later that night, when his mother is tucking him in, he comments, "That was the best movie I've ever seen."

"What movie?" asks his mother.

"That one in the car," he replies.

"But that wasn't a movie," explains his mother, "that was an audio recording."

"Really?" responds the boy. "But I saw the whole thing in my head!" This boy has demonstrated the amazing ability of the mind's eye to create images from text—the power to visualize.

Visualizing and connecting are very closely related. These, above all other strategies, call upon the reader to draw from their own experiences to help make sense of the text. Whether making a connection or making a picture in one's mind, the source from which one connects or creates images is one's well of experiences, one's Memory Pocket (see page 46). Visualizing is the sister to imagination; one could argue that they are one and the same. The source from which the images are created is the only difference. When we use our imaginations, the source for the images created comes from within; when we visualize, the source for the images created comes from the text.

Visualizing is not difficult to do. I believe all children have the ability to close their eyes and imagine or make pictures in their heads. Unfortunately, with the amount of TV viewing in many of our students' homes, the visualizing function in the brain might be in need of some exercise! The problem can also arise, as it does when teaching and practicing connecting, with some readers' lack of experiences; e.g., it is difficult to visualize a beach when one has never been to the beach. When teaching and practicing visualizing with children, it is important to choose books that describe things that your students will be familiar with, so that the images they create come easily. Second Language Learners might require some pre-reading language or vocabulary building so that they have a fuller portfolio of images on which to draw when they begin to visualize. Most of the books used when teaching and practicing this strategy are very descriptive, filled with rich, descriptive, and poetic language that helps the reader create mental images easily. Books that describe weather, seasons, or specific places or things tend to work best.

When readers visualize...

- they are using the words they hear or read in a text to create visual images or "movies in the mind" (Harvey & Goudvis, p. 11).
- they activate their Brain Pockets, or schema, to access their images.
- they are making connections while they visualize.
- they are training their brains for when they begin to read books that don't include pictures with the text.
- they combine their own background knowledge with the words of the author to create mental images that enhance understanding of the text and bring reading to life.
- they are able to activate all their senses to create mental images.
- it is most likely when reading books about places, weather, or seasons that are filled with rich, descriptive, and vivid language.

New Thinking about Visualizing

"Teach two strategies back-to-back in a gradual release way, but then ask students to compare the strengths and weaknesses of each (and as compared with other [strategies] already taught and practiced) with different texts, to make clear that flexible self-prompted use is the aim."
—Grant Wiggins (blogpost)

Over years of teaching Reading Power, I have come to understand how all thinking strategies interact with each other. While we initially isolate them to teach them, in reality they merge together intermittently while we read. When I wrote the first edition of this book, I presented the strategies in an order based on the one David Pearson used in his research (see page 9). I have since, however, changed the order that I teach them. Connecting and Visualizing emerge from almost the same place in our thinking: we draw on personal experiences for both our connections and our visual images. Like connecting, visualization is difficult with something we have not experienced. It is important, therefore, to teach these two reading powers back-to-back, modeling to the students how closely they are linked.

Something else I have discovered about visualizing is that some children struggle with trying to create visual images with their eyes closed. Whenever I read stories and asked children to "close your eyes and visualize," some were not able to. One boy said to me once, "But all I see is black!" I have since given children the option of keeping their eyes open and focusing on a spot in front of them.

Sequential Lessons for Visualizing

Lesson 1 (Teacher Directed): Introducing the Power to Visualize

When there are no pictures in the book, you have to make pictures in your head.

To begin students visualizing, I explain what visualizing is, take them through a series of quick visualizing exercises, then follow with a longer activity. These lessons illustrate four important points:

1. Visualizing is relatively simple to do.
2. "Picture words" help readers visualize.
3. The pictures we make in our heads are created from our own experiences, similar to when we make connections. We often find "pictures" in our memory pockets when we visualize.
4. Visualizing involves not only things we see in our mind, but also our other senses.

I like to make the comparison of an artist painting a picture with paints to an author painting a picture with words—one picture we see with our eyes, the other we see with our brain.

- Refer to the Reading Powers Model and place the *Visualize* piece inside the head. Tell students they will be learning another way active readers think about what they are reading.
- Write the word *Visualize* on the board or interactive whiteboard. Tell students that the word comes from the word *vision* which means "to see." Explain that when readers visualize, they are not using their eyes to see a picture, but instead they are using their brain to make a picture—it's a thinking picture rather than a real picture. "You don't use your EYES when you VISUALIZE!"
- Tell students that most people already know how to visualize and that you are going to do some quick visualizing exercises.

QUICK VISUALIZING EXERCISES

- Explain that you are going to say a word, and ask students to make a picture in their heads of that word. Start out with a simple noun such as "rainbow." Invite students to visualize with their eyes closed or open and staring at one spot in the distance. Give students a few seconds to visualize, then ask them who had a picture of a rainbow in their heads. Most students are able to do this without too much difficulty.
- Move on to other terms; e.g., "ice cream cone," "pencil crayons," "dog." After each, have students pair up and share their images: *What flavor was your ice cream? What kind of dog did you visualize?*
- For an interesting challenge, use adverbs and adjectives, such as "freezing," "slowly," or "scary," for students to try to visualize. These words will evoke a variety of images from different students, so I like to have students share and compare their thinking pictures with a partner. For example, I might describe my visual image for the work *slowly* like this: *My* slowly *is a snail sliding slowly along the sidewalk and leaving a slimy trail behind it.*
- Then, complicate the exercise by using a word that does not evoke a simple image; e.g., "the," "do," "at."
- After a few of these words, ask students which words were easier to visualize. Explain to the students that not all words help readers visualize, but certain words we call "picture words" will really help them to make their pictures clearly. It is important for readers to pay attention to picture words to help them visualize.

- I introduce the activity the same way for all students:

> I'm going to tell you a story and, while I'm telling the story, I'd like you to close your eyes and visualize. See if you can make a picture or a movie in your mind while you listen to the story. Then we're going to talk about the pictures you made. Everybody, close your eyes and remember that when you are visualizing, the only part of your body that should be moving is your brain. Here we go…

Younger students tend to act out the story as it is read, so it is important to stress to them that when we visualize, the only part of our body that moves is our brains.

- Use this "story" for Primary students to visualize.

> I want you to visualize a lollipop. This lollipop is on a white stick and it has a wrapper on it. Visualize yourself holding this lollipop. I want you to notice the color and shape and size of this lollipop. Some lollipops are big, and some are small; some are round and some are flat —what does yours look like? Now I want you to visualize yourself taking off the wrapper. Listen to the sound as you take the wrapper off. Put the wrapper in the garbage. Now I would like you to visualize yourself taking a lick of the lollipop. What flavor is your lollipop? Take another lick. Now put the lollipop, if it's not too big, in your mouth. Suck on it for a while. Listen to the sound it makes when it hits your teeth. Now take a bite. Listen to the sound the bite makes. Now crunch your lollipop and really get the flavor in your mouth. Some of the candy sticks in your teeth. Now visualize yourself as you take the lollipop out of your mouth. Look at what is left on your stick. Open your eyes.

- For Intermediate students, the school setting and element of mystery require more complex visualizing.

> It is recess time. I want you to visualize yourself outside somewhere on the school playground or school grounds. Where are you? Take a moment to look around you. What can you see from where you are standing? What sounds can you hear? What is the weather like? Visualize yourself eating a recess snack. Take a bite. What are you tasting right now? Keep eating your snack. Suddenly you hear someone calling your name. Visualize yourself looking around to try to locate where the sound is coming from. You suddenly see someone you know very well running towards you. The person is calling your name and has something in his or her hands. This person reaches you, talking very quickly and seeming very excited to show you what is in his or her hands. The person shows you and tells you about it. You ask if you can hold it. Visualize yourself holding the object. Now someone else comes to join you and you all look at this thing. Suddenly, the bell rings. Visualize yourself running with your friends to the nearest door and walk towards your classroom. Open your eyes.

Ask the following questions:

- Who had a movie in their heads while I told that story?
- Who had a colored movie? Whose movie was black and white?
- Who had sounds in their movie? Tastes? Feelings?

- Point out to the students that, although it's called "visualizing," it is not just about things we see. When we visualize, we are actually using all five senses: sights, sounds, tastes, touch, and smells.
- Write the following questions on a chart stand. Have students find partners to share the following information:

Primary	Intermediate
1. What color was your lollipop? 2. What size? 3. What shape? 4. What flavor? 5. After you took a bite, what did your lollipop look like?	1. Where were you on the playground? 2. What was the weather like? 3. What was your recess snack? 4. What sounds could you hear? 5. Who was calling your name? 6. What object did the person show you?

- After this sharing time, continue:

  Raise your hand if you and your partner had exactly the same size, shape, color, and flavor of lollipop? (same place, snack, person, and object?)

  (Occasionally, partners have similar answers, but generally speaking the "mind movies" are all different because the students naturally visualize from their own experiences.)

  Well, that is very interesting. But how could it be that everyone in the room heard the same story but visualized different things? How can that be possible?"

- It is important to point out to your students the link between connecting and visualizing. This exercise illustrates very clearly the same point that is made when introducing connecting: because we are all different, with different experiences and different memories, each person's visualizing is going to be different. Just as we make connections from our own experiences, we visualize from what we know.
- End the lesson by generating a Visualize Anchor Chart to display in the room.

SAMPLE VISUALIZE ANCHOR CHART

Good Readers Visualize!

When I visualize, I…

- use the "picture words" in the story to help me create pictures in my mind.
- use my own experiences to help
- pay attention to my other senses, like feelings, sounds, smells and tastes

I'm visualizing…
I can see that in my mind…
I'm picturing…
I'm imagining…

Lesson 2 (Teacher Directed): Modeling Visualizing on Paper

- To model the strategy, ask another teacher (or librarian, non-enrolling teacher, administrator) to come into your class to help. Choose a book from the Visualize book list (pages 72–79) . Before reading, remove the book jacket and replace it inside-out so that the cover is blank. Divide the book into 4 sections and mark each section with a sticky note for reference.
- Make a T-chart (four squares) on the board, interactive whiteboard, or chart paper. Number the squares 1 to 4.
- Begin to read the first section of the book slowly. The teacher who is modeling begins to make sketches (quick pics) in box #1 while you read. Students are visualizing in their heads at the same time.
- When the teacher finishes the sketch, ask him or her to write one or two picture words that really helped them visualize.
- Invite the teacher to turn the chart stand around and do a point-and-talk with the picture. Respond to the teacher's drawings with comments: "I like the way you just drew a stick person rather than too many details." "I like the way you filled the whole box with images."
- Repeat this process with the three remaining sections of the story, having the teacher draw in different boxes each time, record picture words, and do a point-and-talk.
- After the story is finished, have students and other teacher predict the title.
- Finally, reveal the cover and title and read the book again, showing the pictures.
- Suggested books for this lesson: *Splish, Splash, Spring* by Jan Carr; *Puddles* by Jonathan London; *When the Relatives Came* or *Snow* by Cynthia Rylant; *The Seashore Book* by Charlotte Zolotow.

Lesson 3 (Guided Group Practice): Visualizing on Paper Together

- Repeat Lesson 2: using chart paper divided into four or a T-chart on the board, but this time, invite four different students come up and have each draw a quick pic in one box. The other students can visualize in their heads while you read.
- After each student draws, ask them to record one or two picture words and share their pictures with the class by doing a point-and-talk.
- Suggested books for this lesson: *My Garden* by Jesse Ostrow (very simple text); *Rain Drop Splash* by Alvin Tresselt; *Silence* by Lemniscates; *Seasons* by John Burningham; *Rabbits and Raindrops* by Jim Arnosky; *In the Small, Small Pond* by Denise Fleming; *Gilberto and the Wind* by Marie Hall Ets; *Rain* by Manya Stojic.

Grade 2 Sample

Lessons 4–5 (Independent Practice): Visualizing on Paper on Your Own

- Give students the Four-Corner Visualizing sheet on page 80 or divide a paper into four.
- Read aloud the book (no cover or pictures showing) and ask students to make quick drawings in box #1 while you read the first part of the book. After you finish, ask them to write one or two picture words that helped them visualize that part of the story.
- Have the students do a point-and-talk with a partner about their first box.
- Continue reading the story, stopping after each section for students to do a point-and-talk with a partner.
- At the end of the story, ask the students to write what they think the title of the book is. Have some students share their ideas with the class
- Reveal the cover and title, and read the story again to the class, this time showing the pictures. Discuss how their images compared to the illustrator's.
- Repeat this lesson the next day using another book to give students another opportunity to listen, visualize, and draw. For older students, I like to use the Story Scenes sheet (page 81) that includes space for recording a short summary of the story as well as a visual image.

Lesson 6 (Independent Practice): Single-Image Visualizing

- Pass out the Single-Image Visualizing sheet from page 82. Plain white paper would also work for this lesson.
- Explain that you will be reading a story and students will be recording their images to create one single picture rather than four smaller quick pics.
- Invite students to add to their picture and include details as you read.
- Students can label their picture with "picture words" or write list of words on the side or bottom of the page.

- You might need to read the text several times to allow students to add details to their sketches.
- Have students share their pictures with a partner, and then allow time to go back to their own pictures to add details and possibly color.
- Have students write their prediction of the title of the book on their pictures. Read the title, and show the students the illustrations from the book.
- Suggested books for this lesson: *My Garden* by Jesse Ostrow (works well for K–1); *My Garden* by Kevin Henkes; *Oh Canada* (photo images to the words of the national anthem) published by Scholastic; *In the Small, Small Pond* by Denise Fleming; *Under and Over the Snow* by Kate Messner; *A Good Night Walk* or *Beach* by Elisha Cooper; *Beach House* by Deanna Caswell.

Lesson 7 (Guided Practice): Introducing Using Your Senses

- Introduce students to the Using Our Senses grid on page 83. Explain that when we read, we not only can see pictures in our heads, but we can also use our other senses to hear sounds, taste tastes, feel objects.
- Reproduce the Using Our Senses grid on chart paper. Read aloud and have students come up and write (or draw) in the boxes when they hear, see, smell, feel, or taste things.
- Discuss how the author helped us "see" the story through different senses.
- Suggested books for this lesson: *Gilberto and the Wind* by Marie Hall Ets; *In November* by Cynthia Rylant; *Wild Child* by Lynn Plourde; *The Hello, Goodbye Window* by Norton Juster; *Hello Ocean* by Pam Munoz Ryan; *Owl Moon* by Jane Yolen; *Night Sounds, Morning Colors* by Rosemary Wells; *Water Is Water* by Miranda Paul; *Blue on Blue* by Dianne White.

Lessons 8–9 (Independent Practice): Using Your Senses to Visualize

Repeat the previous group lesson, but choose a new book and have students work independently on their own papers while you read aloud. Make copies of Using Our Senses on page 83 for this lesson.

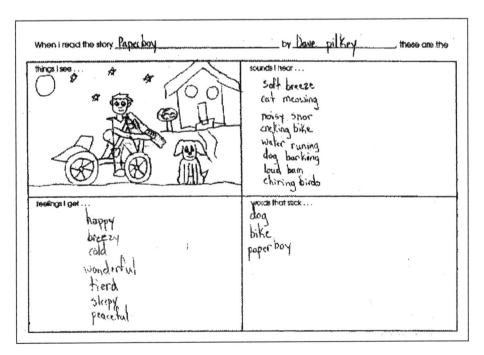

Grade 4 Sample

Lesson 10 (Guided/Independent Practice): Visualizing a Character

- Find a detailed description of a character from a book. Character descriptions from novels work well for this lesson: e.g., description of Willy Wonka from *Charlie and the Chocolate Factory* by Roald Dahl (pp. 60–61).
- Without telling students the name of the book or character, have them visualize the character, then draw and color a detailed picture of the character.
- When everyone is finished, have students display their pictures. Ask, "Why do you think everyone's picture is so similar?" Point out that good writers use such specific picture words when they write that it helps the reader visualize very clearly.
- Have students create their own character and draw it in as much detail as possible. On a separate piece of paper, have them write a description of the created character, including as many picture words as they can think of for size, height, hair/eye/skin color, interesting features, clothes, special objects, etc.
- Collect the completed written descriptions and pass them out randomly.
- Each student reads the description that another student has written and tries to draw a picture of that character. Illustrators then pair up with authors to compare drawings and see how accurately the pictures match their descriptions.

Lesson 11 (Guided/Independent Practice): Draw and Reflect
(adapted from Debbie Miller)

- Choose any book from the Visualize book collection. Read aloud the entire book without showing students the cover or illustrations.
- Ask students to choose one picture they visualized during the story that really stuck in their minds. Using Visualize, Draw, and Reflect #1 or #2 (page 84 or 85), have students draw their images and then write about their choice.
- This lesson can be repeated with students choosing their own books. To avoid copying, have students read through the book a couple of times and then put it back into the book bin. Then have them draw an image from memory.
- Suggested books for this lesson: *What a Wonderful World* by George David Weiss (or play the song as sung by Louis Armstrong); *Baby Beluga* by Raffi; *Following Papa's Song* by Gianna Marino.

Grade 4 Sample

Lessons 12–13 (Independent Practice): Independent Visualizing

- Invite students to chose their own book from the Visualize collection (see book list on pages 77–79) to practice visualizing with. Provide copies of a variety of different templates for them to choose from, including Independent Visualizing (page 86), Story Scenes (page 81), Visualize, Draw, and Reflect (pages 84 and 85), and Listening for Picture Words (page 87).
- As a variation of this exercise, have students sit back to back. One partner reads while the other draws. Afterward, students can discuss the images they drew while reading the book together. Have students switch books and roles, and repeat.

Lesson 13: Reflective Journal

Have students record their thoughts about this new strategy and what they've learned about visualizing. *How has visualizing while you read helped you to understand the story better? Show me or tell me about your thinking.*

Extended Visualize Lessons

- Students use the Listening for Picture Words template on page 87 while reading their own Visualize book.
- Visualizing Poetry: Poetry is a wonderful stimulator of visualized images. Copy the words of a poem onto the template on page 88. Read the poem several times with your students and discuss images they might see. Invite students to draw a picture of what they visualized when reading the poem. Suggested Poems: "Jabberwocky" by Lewis Carroll; "The Wendigo" by Ogden Nash; "Stopping by Woods on a Snowy Evening" by Robert Frost; "Tree House" by Shel Silverstein.
- Visualize a Special Place: Without showing the pictures, read *The Hello, Good-Bye Window* by Norton Juster to students. Discuss how the author describes the grandparent's house with a lot of picture words and includes many senses. Invite the students to draw the scene from the book that was most visual for them—a scene that sticks! Students visualize their own special place (e.g., a room, a park, their bedroom, a tent, the view from a window) and write a descriptive passage about it. Other books for visualizing a special place: *A Quiet Place* by Douglas Wood; *See You Next Year* by Andrew Larsen; *Beach House* by Deanna Caswell; *Blue on Blue* by Dianne White.
- Students choose a descriptive passage in a novel they are reading and create a visual illustration for it.

Visualizing for Older Students

After introducing, modeling, and practicing the strategy of visualizing, use the concept to teach students the literary device of setting and mood. Read excerpts from stories that describe setting in rich, visual detail. Discuss how setting often sets the mood for the story. Explain that mood is how the story makes readers feel like they are part of the setting, whereas tone is the connotation that the author used when writing the piece: in other words, tone is about the author, mood is about the reader.

"Jabberwocky" by Lewis Carroll is a wonderful poem for visualizing with older students. Begin by inviting students to visualize some of the nonsense words from the poem (*slithy toves, Tumtum tree, borogroves*).

For Visualize texts to use with older students, see pages 78–79.

Assessing Visualizing

Because students are recording their visual images through sketches and drawings, we have to be mindful that we are assessing *what* they have recorded rather than *how* they recorded it. This is not about artistic ability, but about how students are able to see with their mind's eye.

ASSESSMENT RUBRIC FOR VISUALIZING

Visualize	NY	M	FM	EX
Is able to visualize independently while reading.				
Demonstrates an ability to visualize either through drawing or oral explanation.				
Identifies key images from the story that enhance understanding.				
Identifies key words or phrases that prompted visualization of images.				
Uses variety of different senses (sight, sound, taste, etc.) when visualizing.				

Visualize Books

P = Primary
I = Intermediate

Once the students are ready to practice visualizing independently, they can choose books from the Visualizing bin. The challenge in independent visualizing is that, when students read independently, they will automatically see the illustrations while they read. I usually tell students to read through the book once, but to put the book back before recording visual images. Choose from the following books to create a collection of Visualizing books for your classroom or library.

BOOKS DESCRIBING A PERSON, PLACE, OR THING

Alborough, Jez. *Watch Out, Big Bro Is Coming!* (P)
Arnosky, Jim. *Rabbits and Raindrops* (P)
Ashman, Linda. *Castles, Caves and Honeycombs* (P, I)
Baker, Keith. *Who Is the Beast?* (P, I)
Brinkloe, Julie. *Fireflies!* (P, I)
Brown, Margaret Wise. *Big Red Barn* (P)
Brown, Ruth. *Imagine* (P, I)
Carroll, Lewis. *Jabberwocky* (P, I)
Cooper, Elisha. *A Goodnight Walk* (P, I)
Cooper, Elisha. *Beach* (P, I)
Cooper, Elisha. *Dance!* (P, I)
Cooper, Elisha. *Farm* (P)
Cottin, Menena. *The Black Book of Colors* (I)
Demers, Dominique. *Every Single Night* (P, I)

Duksta, Laura. *I Love You More* (P)
Fleming, Denise. *In the Small, Small Pond* (P)
Fleming, Denise. *In the Tall, Tall Grass* (P)
Frasier, Debra. *Out of the Ocean* (P, I)
Gerstein, Mordicai. *The Night World* (P, I)
Gorman, Chris. *Indi Surfs* (P, I)
Hamanaka, Sheila. *All the Colors of the Earth* (P, I)
Heidbreder, Robert. *I Wished for a Unicorn* (P, I)
Henderson, Kathy. *The Little Boat* (P)
Henkes, Kevin. *My Garden* (P)
Hundal, Nancy. *Camping* (I)
Jenkins, Emily. *Water in the Park: A Book About Water and Times of the Day* (P, I)
Juster, Norton. *The Hello, Goodbye Window* (P, I)
Larson, Andrew. *See You Next Year* (I)

Lawson, Julie. *Kate's Castle* (I)

Lemniscates. *Silence* (P, I)

Lester, Alison. *Imagine* (P, I)

Liao, Jimmy. *The Sound of Colors* (I)

London, Jonathan. *Giving Thanks* (P, I)

MacLachlan, Patricia. *All the Places to Love* (P, I)

Maclear, Kyo. *The Specific Ocean* (I)

Marino, Gianna. *Following Papa's Song* (P)

Messner, Kate. *Under and Over the Snow* (P, I)

Morris, Jackie. *Tell Me a Dragon* (P, I)

Ostrow, Jesse. *My Garden* (P)

Pilkey, Dav. *The Paperboy* (I)

Reid, Barbara. *Picture a Tree* (P, I)

Ryan, Pam Munoz. *Hello Ocean* (P, I)

Ryder, Joanne. *Chipmunk Song.*(P, I)

Ryder, Joanne. *The Snail's Spell* (P, I)

Ryder, Joanne. *The Waterfall's Gift* (I)

Scanlon, Liz Garton. *All the World* (P, I)

Sidman, Joyce. *Swirl by Swirl: Spirals in Nature* (P, I)

Showers, Paul. *The Listening Walk* (P, I)

St. Pierre, Stephanie. *What the Sea Saw* (P, I)

Stringer, Lauren. *Winter Is the Warmest Season* (P, I)

Thomson, Sarah L. *Imagine a Day* (I)

Thomson, Sarah L. *Imagine a Night* (I)

Thomson, Sarah L. *Imagine a Place* (I)

Thomson, Sarah L. *Imagine a World* (I)

Thong, Roseanne. *Round Is a Mooncake* (P)

Underwood, Deborah. *The Quiet Book* (P)

Van Dusen, Chris. *If I Built a House* (I)

Vivian, Bart. *Imagine* (P, I)

Weiss, George David. *What a Wonderful World* (P)

Wells, Rosemary. *Night Sounds, Morning Colors* (P, I)

White, Dianne. *Blue on Blue* (P, I)

Willis, Jeanne. *Mole's Sunrise* (P, I)

Yolen, Jane. *Owl Moon* (P, I)

Young, Ed. *Should You Be a River* (I)

Zolotow, Charlotte. *The Seashore Book* (P, I)

BOOKS DESCRIBING WEATHER AND SEASONS

Ashman, Linda. *Rain!* (P)

Brett, Jan. *Who's That Knocking on Christmas Eve?* (P, I)

Brown, Margaret Wise. *Goodnight Songs: A Celebration of the Seasons* (P, I)

Burningham, John. *Seasons* (P)

Carlstrom, Nancy White. *The Snow Speaks* (I)

Carr, Jan. *Splish, Splash, Spring* (P)

Chase, Edith Newlin. *Waters* (P)

Chernesky, Felicia Sanzari. *Sugar White Snow and Evergreens: A Winter Wonderland of Color* (P, I)

Ets, Marie Hall. *Gilberto and the Wind* (P)

Fitch, Sheree. *No Two Snowflakes* (P, I)

Fleming, Denise. *The First Day of Winter.* (P)

Fogliano, Julie. *And Then It's Spring* (P, I)

Frost, Robert; Susan Jeffers (ill.). *Stopping by Woods on a Snowy Evening* (I)

Gerber, Carole. *Winter Trees* (P, I)

Gill, Deirdre. *Outside* (P)

Heidbreder, Robert. *Song for a Summer Night* (P, I)

Hubbell, Patricia. *Snow Happy!* (P)

Hundal, Nancy. *November Boots* (P, I)

Johnston, Tony. *Winter is Coming* (I)

Keats, Ezra Jack. *The Snowy Day* (P)

London, Jonathan. *Puddles* (P, I)

Milbourne, Anna. *The Windy Day* (P, I)

Na, Il Sung. *Snow Rabbit, Spring Rabbit: A Book of Changing Seasons* (P)

Patterson, Heather. *Thanks for Thanksgiving* (P)

Plourde, Lynn. *Wild Child* (P, I)

Rocco, John. *Blizzard* (P, I)

Rylant, Cynthia. *In November.* (I)

Rylant, Cynthia. *Snow* (P, I)

Ray, Mary Lyn. *Mud.* (P, I)

Ray, Mary Lyn. *Red Rubber Boot Day* (P, I)

Sidman, Joyce. *Winter Bees and Other Poems of the Cold* (I)

Spinelli, Eileen. *Here Comes the Year* (I)

Stojic, Manya. *Rain* (P, I)

Wong, Herbert Yee. *Summer Days and Nights* (P)

Wong, Herbert Yee. *Who Likes Rain?* (P)

Zolotow, Charlotte. *The Storm Book* (P, I)

BOOKS WITH ABORIGINAL THEMES

Flett, Julie. *Wild Berries* (P, I)

Hainnu, Rebecca and Ziegler, Anna. *A Walk on the Tundra* (P, I)

Highway, Tomson. *Fox On the Ice: Maageesees Maskwameek Kaapit* (P, I)

McLeod, Elaine. *Lessons From Mother Earth* (P)

Waboose, Jan Bourdeau. *Morning on the Lake* (P, I)

Waboose, Jan Bourdeau. *SkySisters* (I)

VISUALIZE TEXTS FOR OLDER STUDENTS (GRADES 8–12)

Boyden, Joseph. *Three Day Road* (*strong content)

Brant, Beth. "Swimming Upstream" (short story)

Carroll, Lewis. "Jabberwocky" (poem)

Cottin, Manena; Rosana Faria (ill.); *The Black Book of Colours* (picture book)

Lessing, Doris. "A Sunrise on the Veld" (short story)

Noyes, Alfred. "The Highway Man" (poem)

O'Flaherty, Liam. "The Wounded Cormorant" (short story)

Plourde, Lynn. *Wild Child* (picture book)

Ross, Sinclair. "The Painted Door" (short story)

Tellez, Hernando. "Ashes for the Wind" (short story)

Tolkien, J.R.R. *The Hobbit* (Chapter 8: Flies and Spiders)

Four-Corner Visualizing

Name: _____   Date: _____

1.	2
3.	4.

I think the title of this book is _____

The actual title of the book is _____

Pembroke Publishers © 2015 *Reading Power, Revised and Expanded* by Adrienne Gear ISBN 978-1-55138-310-1

Story Scenes

Name: _____   Date: _____

In the story…	What I visualized…
_____ _____ _____ _____ _____	
_____ _____ _____ _____ _____	
_____ _____ _____ _____ _____	

Pembroke Publishers © 2015 *Reading Power, Revised and Expanded* by Adrienne Gear ISBN 978-1-55138-310-1

Single-Image Visualizing

Name: _____   Date: _____

Title: _____   Author: _____

Choose one part or scene from the story that you "saw" in your mind. Draw a picture of what you visualized.

Describe your picture in detail.
In this part of the story, I saw…

_____

_____

_____

_____

_____

Pembroke Publishers © 2015 *Reading Power, Revised and Expanded* by Adrienne Gear ISBN 978-1-55138-310-1

Using Our Senses

Name: _____ Date: _____

when I read the story _____ by _____ these are the...

things I see:	sounds I hear:
feelings I get:	words that stick:

Pembroke Publishers © 2015 *Reading Power, Revised and Expanded* by Adrienne Gear ISBN 978-1-55138-310-1

Visualize, Draw, and Reflect #1

Name: _____

Date: _____

Title: _____

Pembroke Publishers © 2015 *Reading Power, Revised and Expanded* by Adrienne Gear ISBN 978-1-55138-310-1

Visualize, Draw, and Reflect #2

Name: _____ Date: _____

When I read the story_____ by_____

these are the pictures I see in my mind…

1.	2.

3.	4.

Pembroke Publishers © 2015 *Reading Power, Revised and Expanded* by Adrienne Gear ISBN 978-1-55138-310-1

Independent Visualizing

Name: _____   Date: _____

Title: _____   Author: _____

PICTURES I SEE	PICTURE WORDS
	_____ ⬜
	_____
	_____
	_____
	_____
	_____
SENSES Sounds/Smells/Tastes:	**CONNECTIONS** What does this story remind you of?
_____	_____
_____	_____
_____	_____
_____	_____
_____	_____

Reflection: Was this a good book for visualizing? Explain.

_____

_____

_____

Pembroke Publishers © 2015 *Reading Power, Revised and Expanded* by Adrienne Gear ISBN 978-1-55138-310-1

Listening for Picture Words

Name: _____   Date: _____

Title: _____   Author: _____

While you read…
Visualize the story. Listen for words that help you make pictures in your mind.

After you read…
Draw one of the pictures that you visualized. Around the picture, write the picture words the author used to help you make the picture.

Visualizing Poetry

Name: _____   Date: _____

Read the poem. Draw a picture of a scene that you **visualize** from the poem.

Title: _____

Copy/paste poem below.

5 The Power to Question

Question Song
(to the tune of "Oh My Darling, Clementine")

Chorus:
Oh I wonder,
Oh I wonder,
Oh I wonder while I read.
All good readers ask deep questions
And they wonder while they read.

Sometimes when I ask a question
And I turn the page to look,
I find the answer to my question
And it's right there in the book.

But sometimes I can't find the answer
Even when the story's read.
So I have to find the answer
To the question—in my head!

(Repeat Chorus)

✳ ✳ ✳

"The answers aren't important really. What's important is knowing all the questions."
—Z.K. Snyder, *The Changeling*

Reading random passages and answering comprehension questions were standard exercises when I was in school. When I was in Grade 7, we did "reading comprehension" twice a week. Reading in my class was working through an SRA kit—that wonderful compact neatly-organized box filled with shiny color-coded cards filled with random passages. Each card had a narrow black-and-white drawing at the top and the story below, followed by ten questions on the back. The cards were leveled by colors and we worked our way methodically through each of the stories of one color and then moved into the next set of colors. If my memory serves me correctly, the colors at the front of the box, at the lowest reading level, were muddy tones with rather unpleasant names: tan, rust, gray, mustard. The colors towards the back of the box were far more appealing: magenta, aquamarine, goldenrod.

Reading on Tuesday and Thursday afternoons looked like this: One row at a time, we each would go up to the SRA kit and select our card. I returned to my seat to quietly read the story and answer the ten questions in my notebook in complete sentences. When complete, I would bring my notebook up to the teacher's desk to be marked. The teacher marked the answers. If I had answered the questions correctly, she stamped my book loudly and announced to the class the color I was moving on to: "Adrienne Gear has just moved up to *Mustard #3*!" Everyone would stop working and watch as I walked proudly back to the SRA kit and changed my card. Then I sat back at my desk to begin the process again. If I went up to the teacher's desk and did not get a stamp and announcement, the silence echoed and all eyes followed as I did the walk of shame back to my desk to do the dreaded corrections.

Most of the questions on the SRA cards were literal questions. I discovered rather early in this process—as many children do—that I, in fact, did not actually have to read the story in order to be able to answer most of the questions. I just found the answer right in the text, turned the question into a statement answer and moved on to the next question. But the questions usually saved for the end were not literal. They were the *What if…?*, *Why…?*, *Why do you think…?* questions. Those answers, no matter how hard I looked, were not anywhere to be found on the card. I consistently struggled with those questions, not only because I hadn't actually read the story but, I now realize, also because nobody showed me how to answer them. I was never taught that answers that are not right there in the text need to come from me. These are the questions that take us deeper into the story and really demonstrate whether understanding has taken place. But I wanted the "right" answer—the answer I could find in the book—and I was not confident enough to rely on my own thinking to find the answers to those questions within myself. It goes without saying that I spent my Grade 7 year stuck in Mustard. I never made it up to those coveted Goldenrod cards, no matter how much I longed to hear my teacher's loud stamp on my notebook.

As with so much of Reading Power, the strategy of Questioning is deeply rooted in the memory of my experience in that Grade 7 class. My struggle with inferential questions stemmed from a lack of modeling and instruction. Therefore, I want to ensure that students are supported—not only in being able to answer questions that require thinking beyond the surface of the story, but in their ability to ask them as well.

Certainly, when I first began teaching, I was like my Grade 7 teacher, an assign-and-assess instructor: "Read this and answer these questions." I loved a teacher's guide with all the answers provided because it made the assessing part quick and easy. The *Answers Will Vary* questions were less convenient, because they meant I really had to read the student's answer carefully. But now I realize that, if we are to help our students become confident strategic thinkers and learners, it is imperative that the questions we ask encourage them to go beyond the literal surface of the story to a place where thinking is nurtured. So, too, do we need to encourage them to wonder while they read. Answering comprehension questions at the end of a chapter does not encourage wonderment and deep thinking; teaching students to ask questions that reach beyond the surface of the story does.

"No one questions, wonders, no one examines like children. It is not simply that children love questions, but that they live questions."
—Christopher Phillips, *The Philosopher's Club*

When readers ask questions…

- they are learning the power of asking, as well as answering, questions.
- they are becoming curious readers.
- questions are relevant and connected to the meaning of the story.
- they know the difference between quick and deep-thinking questions.
- not all questions will have answers, but often unanswered questions invite the most thinking.
- they are practicing what their (Reading) Power-ful brains are already capable of doing—asking questions.

New Thinking about Questioning

Although it is common practice to stop mid-story while reading aloud and ask students prompting questions, it is important that we refrain from doing this and allow the questions to come from students.

As I mentioned in the previous chapter, one of the biggest shifts in understanding that has emerged since I began teaching Reading Power strategies is my realization of how closely tied the strategies are: connecting with visualizing; questioning with inferring. And because of this new thinking, I now teach the strategies in an order that allows the paired strategies to be taught back-to-back. Questioning and inferring are so closely tied together that they merge during the thinking process. When readers wonder about something about a story that isn't directly answered by the author, their natural instinct is to shift to *maybe* mode and start to infer. Proficient readers naturally do this, but are not necessarily aware of what they are doing. By teaching Infer immediately after Question, we can model how these two strategies come together in our thinking.

Questions that Matter

While reading a story about a homeless man and a young girl who helps him by bringing him warm socks and mittens, a student asks, "Do homeless people snore?" While this student might be interested in this minor detail about the sleeping patterns of the homeless, the question does not deepen his understanding of the story. Just as we notice children making connections that don't enhance understanding, the same falls true with the strategy of asking questions. Children often ask questions that are not relevant to meaning and, like random connections, result in a departure from the meaning of the story. While one could claim they were "deep-thinking questions" because the answer was not found directly in the text, the question itself does not enhance meaning. Questions that matter extend our thinking and enhance understanding, and it's important that we model the difference to our students.

I have noticed how challenging it can be for younger students to actually formulate a question. Perhaps, because they are so used to us asking them questions, they often make statements that begin with "I think…" instead of asking "I wonder…" As with any new concept, children need practice and guidance to learn and improve.

So an aspect of the questioning strategy is guiding students to ask relevant and meaningful questions, rather than random or completely off-topic ones. I have designed new lessons that I hope will help you guide your students in asking more thoughtful questions that target meaning rather than irrelevant details.

Quick and Deep-Thinking Questions

Prior to working through lessons to model the Question strategy, I spend time immersing students in the concept of questions. Interestingly enough, when asked what question words they know, most students come up with the classic

Who? What? Where? When? Why? To get beyond the *W*s, have the class brainstorm other question words, and then leave these up in the classroom for reference (see Questioning Words chart on page 93).

It is also important to introduce students to the two types of questions that good readers (and good thinkers) ask while they read. There are many different terms for these two types of questions: literal and inferential; thick and thin (Harvey & Goudvis, pp. 89, 90); *right-there* and *in-your-head*. I have termed them *quick questions* and *deep-thinking questions* (see Questioning Words chart on page 93). Whichever term you choose to use, I believe children need to be introduced to the idea: *Good readers ask questions while they read; some answers can be found right in the story, but if you can't find the answer in the story, the answer has to come from you.* Again, it is this reinforcement of metacognition—awareness of thinking, of understanding, of questioning and answering—that empowers students to become more confident constructors of meaning. Awareness leads to understanding and asking questions drives our thinking forward.

Sequential Lessons for Questioning

Lesson 1 (Teacher Directed): Introducing the Power to Question

- Using the Reading Powers Model, add the Question puzzle-piece to the child's head.
- Explain that good readers ask questions before they read, while they read, and after they read (see Before, During, and After on page 102 or What Are You Wondering? on page 104).
- Explain that readers ask different types of questions when they read; some questions they ask get answered in the text and some don't.
- Write *Quick Questions* and *Deep-Thinking Questions* at the top of a piece of chart paper or on the interactive whiteboard. (See chart page 93.)
- Explain that sometimes readers ask a question while reading, but as they keep on reading, they find the answer in the story. These are called quick questions, and there is usually only one answer. Once you know the answer to the question, your thinking stops.
- Explain that there are other questions a reader asks that are not answered in the story. These are called deep-thinking questions. If a reader doesn't find the answer to the question in the story, he/she needs to keep on thinking about it—his/her thinking keeps going. These are questions that often lead to a deeper understanding of the story.

> A good reader starts asking questions even before they start reading; and keeps asking questions even after the story ends.

Quick Questions	Deep-Thinking Questions
• Answer found in the book • Usually one "right" answer • Your thinking stops	• Answer NOT found in the book • Answer is from your thinking • Many different answers • Your thinking keeps going!

Lesson 2 (Teacher Directed): Exploring Deep-Thinking Questions

- Remind students about quick and deep-thinking questions.
- Practice asking students some "quick" questions: e.g., "What school do you go to?" "Who is your principal?" "When is your birthday?" "What is your age?"
- Record some of the quick question words—*What*, *Who*, *When*—on a chart (see chart page 93). Remind students that once you know the answer to a quick question, your thinking stops.
- Practice asking some deep-thinking questions: e.g., "Why do you yawn when you see someone yawn?" "Can dogs understand us?" "How do spiders know how to spin webs?"
- Record some of the deep-thinking question words—*Why*, *How*, *Can*—on the chart.
- Ask students how they would answer a question when they don't know the answer: *ask someone else, look on the Internet, think about it.*
- Tell students that their schema, or Brain Pockets, can help them answer questions (see page 46): *What do you already know about this? Go to where you know.*
- Choose one or two books to help illustrate the notion of deep-thinking questions to read aloud to the class: *I Wonder Why* by Lois Rock or *I Wonder* by Tana Hoban (Primary); *The Philosophers' Club* by Christopher Phillips or *Questions, Questions* by Marcus Pfister (Intermediate). (See full list on pages 99–100.)
- Invite students to write a list of things they are wondering about the world. After sharing their list with a partner, ask them to choose one and illustrate it. Use the *I Wonder…* Template on page 101. Make a class book of deep-thinking questions.

When we are practicing deep thinking, I like to invite younger students to find their "deep-thinking pose": head tilted; hand on chin; saying, "Hmmm…"

Grade 3 Sample

Quick Question Words	Deep-thinking Question Words
Who?	Why?
What?	I wonder…
Where?	What if…?
When?	Why do you think…?
What time?	How do you think…?
How old?	

SAMPLE QUESTIONING ANCHOR CHART

Good Readers Ask Questions!
What are you wondering?

When I read, I might wonder about…

- what's happening in the story
- what's going to happen
- why something happened
- a character

I wonder why…?	*Who…?*
How…?	*What…?*
Why do you think…?	*Where…?*
Could…?	*When…?*
Shouldn't…?	*What if…?*
What if…?	*I wonder why…?*
How come…?	

Lessons 3-4 (Teacher Directed): Group Questioning

- Choose one of the Question books from the list on pages 99–100 for modeling.
- Ask questions aloud as you read, marking your questions with sticky notes or directly onto a chart or the interactive whiteboard.
- On chart paper or the board, create a three-column chart: *Quick Questions* (answered in the text); *Deep-Thinking Questions* (not answered in the text); and *Not Connected* (the question doesn't really matter to the story).
- Go through each question, peeling the notes off the text and sticking them to the chart or checking off the appropriate column. Discuss the fact that questions that did not get answered in the text (deep-thinking questions) are often the ones that encourage us to think.
- Divide the class into groups and give each group a deep-thinking question from the chart. Have students discuss the answers. This could be done as a carousel activity: a different deep-thinking question from the story is written on the top of one of several posted chart-sized papers; groups of students rotate to each question, recording their answers on the charts.
- Repeat lesson next day using a different book.
- Suggested books for this lesson: *The Wednesday Surprise* by Eve Bunting; *Charlie Anderson* by Barbara Abercrombie; *Sami and the Time of the Troubles* by Florence Parry Heide; *The Jupiter Stone* by Paul Owen Lewis.

Lesson 5 (Teacher Guided): Asking Questions That Matter

- Use the BIBB strategy (see page 51) for questioning to help guide students to remain focused on the meaning of the story. If a student asks a question that is not connected to the meaning of the story, stop and ask them: *What is this story about? Has your question helped you understand the story better?*
- Explain that not all questions help us understand a story better.
- Tell students you are going to read a story and model some questions.

  Some of those questions will help you go deeper into the story and help you understand it, and some won't.

- Establish a code (e.g., snapping fingers if the question is quick; tapping head if the question is deep-thinking) for whether questions matter to the meaning of the story or not.
- Read and wonder aloud, modeling both questions that matter and those that don't. Invite students to explain why or why not a question might make a difference to the meaning.

The Day Eddie Met the Author by Louise Borden is a wonderful anchor for teaching students about asking questions that matter. While many of his classmates ask a visiting author irrelevant questions ("How old are you?" "Do you have a cat?"), Eddie asks a poignant one: "How do you write stories that have parts meant for me?"

- The following day, remind students that not all questions we ask help us understand a story better. Choose a different book from the Questioning list.
- Students can use the Quick and Deep-Thinking Questions template on page 103 to record their questions as they read, and then decide if questions mattered to the meaning of the story.

Lesson 6 (Guided/Independent): Asking and Answering Quick and Deep-Thinking Questions

- Remind students of the difference between a quick question (answer is found in the text) and a deep-thinking question (answer comes from our thinking). Pass out copies of the Quick and Deep-Thinking Questions template (page 103).
- Choose a book from the Question collection. Begin to read and model, asking one quick and one deep-thinking question. Record the question on a chart or the interactive whiteboard.
- Remind students of the difference between how we answer a quick question and how we answer a deep-thinking question. If the answer is found in the story, the answer needs to be written in the form of a statement: e.g., Q: What was the boy's name; A: The boy's name was Zac. If the answer is not found directly in the the book, the answer will need to begin with "I think…" or "Maybe…".
- Students can chose their own book and complete the template.

Title: How to Heal a Broken wing   Name: Adrian

My "quick question"…

Why did Will pick up the feather?

Answer:
So Will can ask his dad to put the feather back, but dad say to Will the feather can't go back.

My "deep-thinking" question…

Will Will see the bird again?

Answer:
Maybe… he will never see the bird again. The bird is free and happy I think.

Grade 3 Sample

Lessons 7–8 (Guided Practice): Your Turn to Question

- Choose a story from the Question list.
- Give each student three or four sticky notes. Explain to students that while you are reading you would like them to "pay attention to their thinking." Each time they wonder something about the story, they can write the question on one of

the stickies and come up to stick it in the book. You can record questions on chart paper for younger students

- Begin by holding up the book and showing the cover. Explain that good readers start thinking and wondering even before they start reading. Ask students, *What are you wondering about this book?* All students should use the first sticky to ask a question from the cover and title.
- Continue reading, stopping after a few pages (or at a good break point) and ask, *Now what are you wondering about?* If students run out of stickies, tell them they can continue to wonder in their heads.
- Post a chart paper with the columns labeled *Answered in Text: Yes/No* and *Does It Matter?: Yes/No* as in Evaluating Questions on page 105. Proceed through the same routine as in Lesson 5, deciding whether the questions were answered in the story or not and placing the sticky notes in the appropriate column. Repeated questions can be stuck on top of each other.
- Students discuss answers to one or two deep-thinking questions (in pairs or small groups).
- Suggested Primary books for this lesson: *Baby Bear* by Kadir Nelson; *The Storm Whale* by Benjy Davis; *The Egg* by M.P. Robertson. Suggested Intermediate books for this lesson: *Mr. Bear and the Bear* by Frances Thomas; *The Cinder-Eyed Cats* by Eric Rohmann; *Sparrow Girl* by Sara Pennypacker; *Dolphin SOS* by Roy and Slavia Miki.

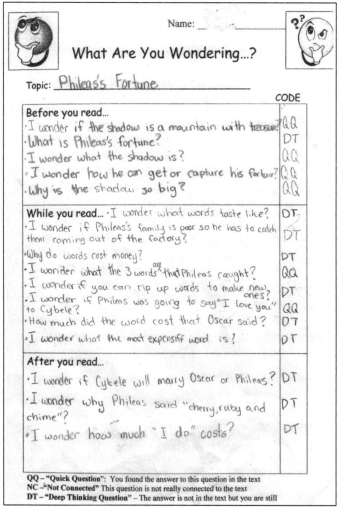

What Are You Wondering...?

Name: _____

Topic: **Phileas's Fortune**

	CODE
Before you read...	
· I wonder if the shadow is a mountain with treasure?	QQ
· What is Phileas's fortune?	DT
· I wonder what the shadow is?	QQ
· I wonder how he can get or capture his fortune?	QQ
· Why is the shadow so big?	QQ
While you read... · I wonder what words taste like?	DT
· I wonder if Phileas's family is poor so he has to catch them coming out of the factory?	DT
· Why do words cost money?	DT
· I wonder what the 3 words are that Phileas caught?	QQ
· I wonder if you can rip up words to make new ones?	DT
· I wonder if Phileas was going to say "I love you" to Cybele?	QQ
· How much did the word cost that Oscar said?	DT
· I wonder what the most expensiff word is?	DT
After you read...	
· I wonder if Cybele will marry Oscar or Phileas?	DT
· I wonder why Phileas said "cherry, ruby and chime"?	DT
· I wonder how much "I do" costs?	DT

QQ – "Quick Question": You found the answer to this question in the text
NC – "Not Connected" This question is not really connected to the text
DT – "Deep Thinking Question" – The answer is not in the text but you are still

Grade 6 Sample

Lessons 9–10 (Independent Practice): Choose Your Own Question Book

- Students choose their own books from the Question books (see Question book list on pages 99–100). While they read, record their questions on sticky notes.
- Have students remove the sticky notes with questions and place them in order down the left side of Evaluating Questions on page 105. They check off whether each of the questions was answered in the story or not.
- Have students choose one of the questions that was not answered in the text and answer this question on the bottom of the page. Encourage students to answer the question using the words "Maybe…" or "I think…"
- Provide several periods for students to choose books from the Question collection to read and practice questioning. Some may want to continue using sticky notes to record their questions, others will record their questions directly onto a questioning sheet: they can use Before, During, and After on page 102, What Are You Wondering? on page 104, or Evaluating Questions on page 105 for these independent lessons.

Lesson 13: Reflective Journal

Have students record their thoughts about this new reading power in their journals. *How does asking questions while you read help you understand the story better? Show me or tell me about your thinking.*

Extended Lessons for Questioning

- Read *If* by Sarah Perry. This book offers readers a collection of strange and imaginative possibilities of how the world could be just a little different: e.g., *What would the world be like… if cats could fly? if the moon were square? if music could be held?* After sharing the book, invite students to choose one of the *Ifs* from the book. Pass out the If… Web on page 106 and have students copy their *If* in the centre box. Students write a question in each of the surrounding six bubbles.
- An option for extending this lesson is to have students create their own *Ifs* and invite classmates to add questions to their page. Papers can be passed and different students can add questions until all six bubbles are filled.

Of the many lessons from the first edition of *Reading Power*, the *If* book and lessons have been the most popular among teachers!

Grade 5 Sample
Book: *If* by Sarah Perry

- Using *The Philosopher's Club* by Christopher Phillips: Choose one of the questions from the book and write it in the centre of a web (see IF... Web on page 106) copied onto large chart paper. Examples: *What is violence? What is silence? Is it possible to be happy and sad at the same time?* Discuss the question with students and model how you might add a response, a reaction, or another question to the web. Over the next few days, invite students to add their own responses to the question. When the web is full, read and share the responses. Compliment your students on their deep thinking.

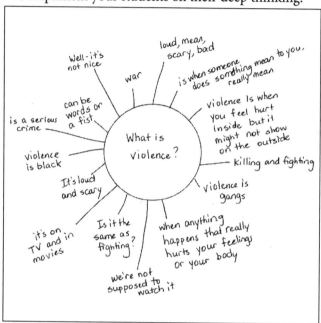

Grade 6/7 Class Responses
Book: *The Philosopher's Club* by Christopher Phillips

- Using *Little Black Crow* by Chris Raschka: After reading *Little Black Crow*, invite students to choose a color and an animal. Using the Little _____ _____ template on page 107, they record a list of questions they would like to ask that animal. Encourage them to include questions about the animals' behavior, habitat, food, family, and feelings.

Questioning for Older Students

After introducing, modeling, and practicing the strategy of questioning, use the concept to teach students the literary device of plot and conflict.

- Explain that the most common questions readers ask about a story are connected to plot: *Why did she do that? What is going to happen to him? What's going to happen next?* While reading a story, model these basic plot questions to create story maps of the rising action, climax, and falling action.
- Explain that the second most common question readers ask about a story is connected to the conflict and how it get resolved. Review the different types of story conflicts: e.g., conflict between two people or groups of people; internal conflict between person and him/herself; conflict between person and their environment. Invite students to identify the different conflicts while you read.

For Question texts to use with older students, see page 100.

Assessing Questions

While it is challenging to assess a child's thinking, there are ways we can evaluate whether or not they demonstrate an understanding of the strategy of questioning, if they can form an effective question independently, and whether or not the questions they are asking enhance meaning and deepen understanding. The rubric below is intended to be used for evaluating this strategy.

ASSESSMENT RUBRIC FOR QUESTIONING

Asking Questions	NY	M	FM	EX
Is able to generate questions independently while reading.				
Demonstrates an understanding of the difference between quick (literal), deep-thinking (thoughtful, relevant), and not-connected (not relevant to meaning of the story) questions.				
Is able to independently generate questions that enhance understanding and are directly related to the meaning of the text.				
Is able to explain how his/her question has helped them understand the text better.				

Question Books

P = Primary
I = Intermediate

Choose from the following books to create a collection of Question books for your classroom. Put aside three to five gem books to use for your modeling lessons.

BOOKS THAT CELEBRATE QUESTIONS

Corderoy, Tracey. *Why?* (P)
Damm, Antje. *Ask Me.* (P, I)
Gay, Marie-Louise. *Stella, Fairy of the Forest* (P, I)
Gay, Marie-Louise. *Stella, Star of the Sea* (P, I)
Gay, Marie-Louise. *Stella, Queen of the Snow* (P, I)
Harris, Annika. *I Wonder* (P, I)
Hoban, Tana. *I Wonder* (P)
Hosford, Kate. *Infinity and Me* (I)
Pfister, Marcus. *Questions, Questions* (P, I)
Phillips, Christopher. *The Philosopher's Club* (I)
Raschka, Chris. *Little Black Crow* (P, I)
Rock, Lois. *I Wonder Why* (P, I)
Torrey, Richard. *Why?* (P)
Torrey, Richard. *Because* (P)
Ziefert, Harriet. *Where Does Kitty Go in the Rain?* (P)

QUESTION BOOKS: REALISTIC

Abercrombie, Barbara. *Charlie Anderson* (I)

Adderson, Caroline. *Norman, Speak!* (I)
Brisson, Pat. *The Summer My Father Was Ten* (I)
Bunting, Eve. *Smoky Nights* (I)
Bunting, Eve. *Fly Away Home* (P, I)
Bunting, Eve. *Gleam and Glow* (I)
Burleigh, Robert. *Trapped! A Whale's Rescue* (P, I)
Campbell, K.G. *The Mermaid and the Shoe* (P, I)
Chinn, Karen. *Sam and the Lucky Money* (P, I)
Cox, Lynne. *Elizabeth, Queen of the Seas* (P, I)
Davis, Benjy. *The Storm Whale* (P, I)
Dubuc, Marianne. *The Lion and the Bird* (P, I)
Garland, Sherry. *The Lotus Seed* (I)
George, Jean Craighead. *The Last Polar Bear* (P, I)
Heide, Florence Parry. *Sami and the Time of the Troubles* (I)
Heide, Florence Parry. *The Day of Ahmed's Secret* (I)
Khadra, Mohammed. *Four Feet, Two Sandals* (I)
Lauthier, Jennifer. *The Stamp Collector* (I)
Leathers, Philippa. *The Black Rabbit* (P, I)

Lodding, Linda Ravin. *A Gift for Mama* (I)

McGovern, Ann. *The Lady in the Box* (I)

Miki, Roy & Slavia. *Dolphin SOS* (I)

Nelson, Kadir. *Baby Bear* (P)

Olshan, Matthew. *The Mighty Lalouche* (I)

Rylant, Cynthia. *An Angel for Solomon Singer* (I)

Stinson, Kathy. *The Man with the Violin* (P, I)

Thomas, Frances. *Mr. Bear and The Bear* (I)

Trottier, Maxine. *Claire's Gift* (I)

Trottier, Maxine. *Dreamstones* (I)

Pennypacker, Sarah. *Sparrow Girl* (I)

Van Allsburg, Chris. *Queen of the Falls* (I)

Wallace, Ian. *Boy of the Deeps* (I)

Wild, Margaret. *Fox* (I)

Willems, Mo. *City Dog, Country Frog* (P, I)

QUESTION BOOKS: FANTASY

Barnett, Mac. *Sam and Dave Dig a Hole* (P, I)

Barnett, Mac. *Billy Twitters and His Blue Whale Problem* (P, I)

Browne, Anthony. *Changes* (P, I)

Catchpool, Michael. *The Cloud Spinner* (I)

Davies, Nicola. *The Promise* (I)

de Lestrade, Agnes. *Phileas's Fortune* (I)

Demers, Dominique. *Old Thomas and the Little Fairy.* (P, I)

DePaola, Tomie. *Strega Nona* (P, I)

Ering, Timothy Basil. *The Story of Frog Belly Rat Bone* (P, I)

Hall, Kristen. *The Jacket* (I)

Harrison, Troon. *The Dream Collector.* (P, I)

Joyce, William. *A Day with Wilbur Robinson.* (P, I)

Lewis, Paul Owen. *The Jupiter Stone* (P, I)

Miyakoshi, Akiko. *The Tea Party in the Woods* (P)

Perry, Sarah. *If* (P, I)

Robertson, M.P. *The Dragon's Egg* (P)

Robertson, M.P. *The Sandcastle* (P)

Rohmann, Eric. *The Cinder-Eyed Cats* (P, I)

Rohmann, Eric. *Clara and Asha.* (P, I)

Rylant, Cynthia. *The Van Gogh Café.* (I)

Santat, Dan. *The Adventures of Beekle: The Imaginary Friend* (P)

Say, Allen. *Stranger in the Mirror* (I)

Snicket, Lemony. *29 Myths on the Swinster Pharmacy* (I)

Soman, David. *Three Bears in a Boat* (P)

Steig, William. *Brave Irene* (P, I)

Steig, William. *Doctor De Soto* (P, I)

Steig, William. *Sylvester and the Magic Pebble* (P, I)

Teague, Mark. *The Lost and Found* (P, I)

Teague, Mark. *The Secret Shortcut* (P, I)

Wargin, Kathy-Jo. *The Legend of the Loon* (I)

BOOKS WITH ABORIGINAL THEMES

Arnaquq-Baril, Alethea. *The Blind Boy and the Loon* (P, I)

Angutingunrik, Jose. *The Giant Bear* (I)

Goodall, Jane. *The Eagle and the Wren* (P, I)

Highway, Tomson. *Caribou Song: Atihko Nikamon* (I)

Isluanik, Henry. *Kiviuq's Journey* (I)

James, Elizabeth. *The Woman Who Married a Bear* (I)

Lewis, Paul Owen. *Frog Girl* (I)

Lewis, Paul Owen. *Storm Boy* (I)

McDermott, Gerald. *Raven: A Trickster Tale from the Pacific Northwest* (P, I)

Nelson, S.D. *The Star People: A Lakota Story* (P, I)

Pendziwol, Jean E. *The Red Sash* (I)

Rafe, Martin. *The Rough-Face Girl* (I)

Simpson, Carroll. *The First Beaver* (P, I)

Simpson, Carroll. *The First Mosquito* (P, I)

Simpson, Carroll. *The Salmon Twins* (P, I)

Simpson, Carroll. *Brothers of the Wolf* (I)

Spalding, Andrea. *Solomon's Tree* (P, I)

Spalding, Andrea. *Secret of the Dance* (I)

Swanson, Bruce. *Gray Wolf's Search* (P, I)

Van Camp, Richard. *A Man Called Raven* (I)

Vaughan, Richard Lee. *Eagle Boy: A Pacific Northwest Native Tale* (I)

Vickers, Roy Henry. *Cloudwalker* (P, I)

Vickers, Roy Henry. *Orca Chief* (P, I)

Vickers, Roy Henry. *Raven Brings the Light* (P, I)

Wargin, Kathy-Jo. *The Voyageur's Paddle* (I)

Williams, Maria. *How Raven Stole the Sun* (P, I)

Yahgulanaas, Michael. *The Little Hummingbird* (P, I)

Yolen, Jane. *Encounter* (I)

QUESTIONTEXTS FOR OLDER STUDENTS (GRADES 8–12)

Asimov, Isaac. "All the Troubles of the World" (short story)

Atwood, Margaret. *Oryx and Crake* (* strong content)

Bradbury, Ray. "The Veldt" (short story)

Coakley, Lena. "Mirror Image" (short story)

Hughes, Monica. "Invitation to the Game" (short story)

Jacobs, W.W. "The Monkey's Paw" (short story)

Pennypacker, Sara. *Sparrow Girl* (picture book)

Perry, Sarah. *If* (picture book)

Poe, Edgar Allan. "The Tell-tale Heart" (short story)

Skarmeta, Antonio. *The Composition* (picture book)

Waddington, Patrick. "The Street that Got Mislaid" (short story)

I Wonder...

Name: _____   Date: _____

Before, During, and After

Name: _____   Date: _____

Good readers **ASK QUESTIONS** before, during, and after they read. Questions help us to think more deeply about what we are reading. Sometimes we can find answers to our questions in the book; other times, we need to use our own thinking to find an answer.

What are you wondering **BEFORE** you read?

_____ ?
_____ ?
_____ ?
_____ ?

What are you wondering **WHILE** you read?

_____ ?

_____ ?

_____ ?

_____ ?

What are you wondering after you read?

_____ ?

_____ ?

_____ ?

Choose one of your questions and try to answer it. What do YOU think?

I think… _____

_____

_____

Pembroke Publishers © 2015 *Reading Power, Revised and Expanded* by Adrienne Gear ISBN 978-1-55138-310-1

Quick and Deep-Thinking Questions

Name: _____   Date: _____

Title: _____

My quick question	My deep-thinking question
_____ _____ Answer: _____ _____ _____	_____ _____ Answer: Maybe… _____ _____ _____
My quick question _____ _____ Answer: _____ _____ _____	My deep-thinking question _____ _____ Answer: Maybe… _____ _____ _____
My quick question _____ _____ Answer: _____ _____ _____	My deep-thinking question… _____ _____ Answer: Maybe… _____ _____ _____

Pembroke Publishers © 2015 *Reading Power, Revised and Expanded* by Adrienne Gear ISBN 978-1-55138-310-1

What Are You Wondering?

Name: _____   Date: _____

Title: _____

Before you read…	Code
While you read…	
After you read…	

QQ = Quick Question: You found the answer to this question right in the text
NC = Not Connected: This question is not really connected to the meaning of the text
DT = Deep-Thinking Question: The answer is not in the text but you are still wondering about it

Pembroke Publishers © 2015 *Reading Power, Revised and Expanded* by Adrienne Gear ISBN 978-1-55138-310-1

Evaluating Questions

Name: _____   Date: _____

Title: _____   Author: _____

Questions we had while we read	Answered in Text		Does it Matter?	
	Yes	No	Yes	No

Choose one of the questions that was not answered in the story but that matters to the story and write what you think.

Question: _____

Answer: I think… _____

Pembroke Publishers © 2015 *Reading Power, Revised and Expanded* by Adrienne Gear ISBN 978-1-55138-310-1

IF… Web

Name: _____

Date: _____

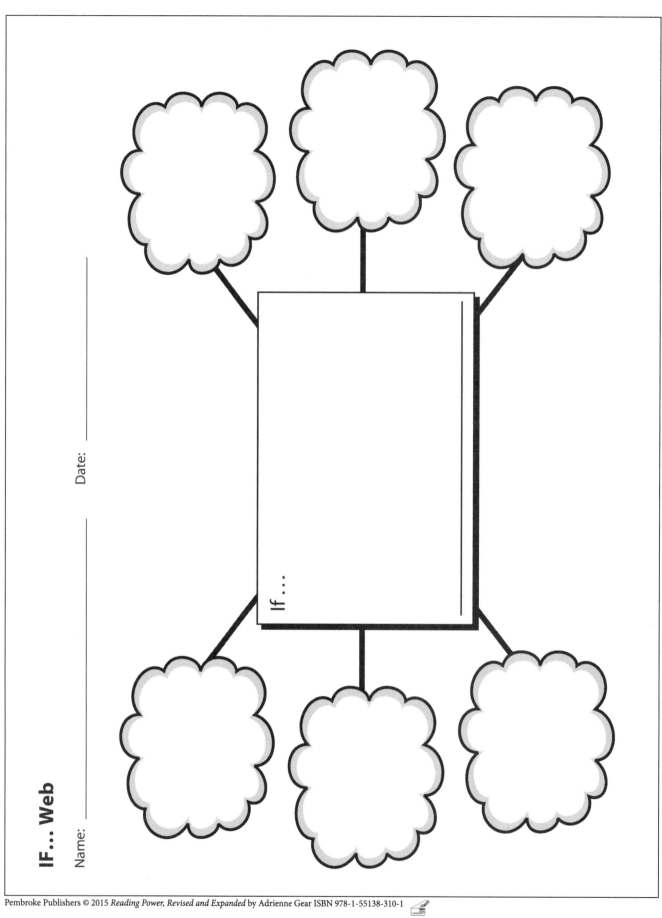

If …

Little _____ _____

Name: _____ Date: _____

If you could talk to that animal or insect, what questions would you want to ask it? Think about such things as what it looks like, how it acts, what it eats, where it lives, its family, feelings, likes, dislikes.

_____

_____

_____

_____

_____

_____

_____

_____

_____

_____

_____

_____

_____

_____

_____

_____

_____

Pembroke Publishers © 2015 *Reading Power, Revised and Expanded* by Adrienne Gear ISBN 978-1-55138-310-1

6 The Power to Infer

Infer Song
(to the tune of "My Bonnie Lies Over the Ocean")

Sometimes when you're reading a story
The words are not all there for you
So being a good book detective
Will help you to find any clue!

Chorus:
Infer! Infer!
Filling in what is not in the book!
Infer! Infer!
It's taking a much closer look!

Some authors leave clues in their pictures.
Some authors leave clues in their text.
They give you just part of their story
And want you to fill in the rest!

(Repeat Chorus)

So when you are reading a story
Be careful to read what is there
But then figure out what is missing—
Now you are inferring with flair!

* * *

"A successful book is not made of what is in it, but of what is left out of it."
—Mark Twain

"Reading between the lines" has become the standard definition for inferring, but this has never been clear enough or concrete enough for me to really understand. Reading between the lines? What is that, exactly? The definition I have found to be more helpful when teaching this strategy is this: Inferring is filling in, in your head, what is not written on the page. Just as the powers to Connect and Visualize are strongly linked, so is the power to Infer is linked to the power to Question. The "in your head, not in the book" thinking introduced with deep-thinking questions is emphasized again with the strategy of inferring: drawing readers' attention to the difference between what they know because the author has written it and what they need to fill in because the author did not include it.

"I read literature slowly, digging for the hidden... eager to envision what is there, noticing what is not."
—Toni Morrison, *The Reader as Artist*

When readers infer...

- they learn to look for clues in text, in pictures, and in their own knowledge that will help them to make sense of the text.
- they are encouraged to become "book detectives."
- they learn that some authors write very little text but leave clues for the reader to discover and interpret.
- they understand that the expression "less is more" means that fewer words on the page means more thinking for the reader.
- they are learning to fill in, in their heads, what's not written on the page.
- they can scaffold their understanding of inferring through pictures and wordless picture books.

Inferring, because of its ties to higher-level thinking, is often a challenging concept for teachers to approach. How do we teach children to think beyond what is actually in the story? As with all the other reading powers and strategies, I believe that children know and are able to make inferences, but that what is going on in their heads has not yet been given a name or been made concrete. My five-year-old son Oliver, seeing the look on my face after he did something naughty, said, "Uh-oh. I'm inferring that I'm in trouble." Then, seeing my "look" quickly changing into a smile, said, "Oh, maybe I inferred wrong." I was smiling because it seemed odd for a five-year-old to be using the word "inferring" in proper context. What became clear to me was how easily Oliver was able to understand and use this language because I'd been modeling it with him—not in a formal lesson, yet intentionally and purposefully integrating this language into his world every opportunity I could.

I like to help students unlock the mystery of inferring by telling them this:

I'm going to tell you a secret that will help you learn to infer. Are you ready? Here's the secret—not all authors tell you everything. But they didn't not tell you everything because they lost their pen or ran out of paper. They didn't tell you everything because they wanted you, the reader, to figure it out for yourself.

Now I'm going to tell you another secret—you already know how to infer! You actually infer every day!

"What I like in a good author is not what he says, but what he whispers."
—Logan Pearsall Smith

(Give students examples of when they infer: e.g., when you see a dog or cat sitting by the back door, you infer the pet wants to go out; when your baby sister or brother is crying, we might infer the child is hungry or tired.)

When words are not spoken, we look for clues and we infer; when words are not written, we look for clues and infer.

As with all the other reading powers, there are books that lend themselves best to teaching and practicing the specific strategy. Books selected to teach visualizing, for example, have been specifically selected because of their rich language and detailed descriptions. But perhaps no other reading power relies quite so much on the specific literature used to model and teach it as inferring does. I believe that many of the books selected to support this strategy are written by perhaps the most talented authors. It is far more challenging to tell a story with few words—to imply rather than tell, to be subtle, to choose how much to actually say and just how much to leave out, to leak out a story in a controlled manner—than to tell everything at once. Authors such as Chris Van Allsburg, Anthony Browne, and David Wiesner are examples of writers who have mastered their craft. These writers tell their stories by *not* telling their stories. It is to these books and to these authors we turn when teaching students how to infer.

Less inking means more thinking.

While developing my book list for the strategy of inferring, I noticed something interesting about the books I was choosing. While close to 80% of the books in the Visualize bin had the writing and illustration done by different people, more than 80% of the books in the Infer bin were written and illustrated by the same person. Why is this? The answer has helped me understand inferring even more. I believe that the authors of the Infer books want to be in full control of both their stories and their pictures. They intentionally want to leak the story slowly and carefully onto the page. Having someone else illustrate their books would be giving up some of that control.

Another excellent tool when teaching readers to infer is the wordless picture book, for what better source is there for "filling in, in your head" than a book with no or very few words? Books by Aaron Becker (*Journey*, *Quest*), Barbara Lehman (*Museum Trip*, *The Red Book*), *Hug* by Jez Alborough, *Yo! Yes!* by Chris Raschka, and *Look!* by Jeff Mack are perfect resources for helping students understand what inferring looks like and feels like. Children have no trouble "reading" the pictures to tell these stories; by naming the process *Inferring*, we take the mystery out of the word and make it more tangible.

Comic books are an excellent tool to use for teaching inferring. Copy one page, whiting out some or all of the text from the speaking or thinking bubbles, and have students infer the conversation. Or remove some of the frames of the comic and invite students to infer what happens between the frames.

There was some controversy at my school a few years ago regarding comic books and graphic novels. Some parents and teachers felt that building up a large collection of comic books in the library promoted poor reading material for children. Our teacher-librarian strongly disagreed. She knew that, while not all comic books and graphic novels are appropriate for school, the ones she was purchasing for the library, such as *Calvin and Hobbs* and *Garfield*, were not only appropriate, but also had reluctant readers, particularly boys, coming into the library on a regular basis and actually reading. In fact, she could rarely keep up with the demands of the students when it came to this genre. Still, the issues surrounding comic books and graphic novels remains, as some still might not view them as "real books."

A study conducted in the United States found that boys who grew up reading comic books had, in fact, excelled in reading as they moved through high school and university. It was suggested that one of the reasons for this was that readers of comic books had already mastered the art of inferring. Comic books and graphic novels demand inferences between every frame. Readers of these books might not be aware that what they are doing is called inferring, but they would certainly be refining this skill by reading comic books on a regular basis. And anyone who works in a school library knows that the graphic novel series such as *Bone*, *Babymouse*, and *Amulet* are the hardest to keep on the shelves.

I agree that inferring is a challenging reading strategy to teach and practice. But by scaffolding thinking by moving from picture to simple text to more complex texts, and by providing many opportunities for students to easily and successfully fill in parts of the story, we can reinforce the strategy and give this cognitive process a name.

New Thinking About Inferring

Are predicting and inferring the same thing? When someone asked me this at a workshop, I did not know the answer, but it certainly started me thinking about it. In some respects, a prediction and an inference are both based on the notion that the reader uses clues to try to figure out an unknown. In the case of a prediction, the unknown is primarily grounded in the plot: "What is going to happen next?" and can be verified as right or wrong once the reader finishes the story. For example, when reading The Three Bears for the first time, a reader might predict that the bears are going to come home and eat Goldilocks. When the story ends, the prediction can be verified—yes, the bears came home but, no, Goldilocks didn't get eaten. When the story ends, we know one way or another if our prediction was accurate.

An inference, on the other hand, is often not verified in the story. For example, the story *Mr. Bear and the Bear* by Frances Thomas begins with a description of a grumpy old man who lives by himself at the top of a hill and never talks to anyone. Readers certainly wonder why he is so grumpy and so might infer that something tragic happened to him or his family. The author never actually tells us why the character ended up this way, but readers are left to think about it and fill in for themselves. I see inferring as being a higher-level strategy than a prediction, because an inference is often not verified by the author. This has helped me to realize that, developmentally, we might start by teaching children how to make a prediction, but we should slowly nudge their thinking towards the more open-ended inference.

Sequential Lessons for Inferring

Lesson 1 (Teacher Directed/Group Participation): Introducing Inferring through Games

- Introduce the word "infer" and explain that inferring is something good readers do to try to figure out what the author is saying, even though the author may not have actually written it down. Explain that good readers are able to infer because they look for clues in the pictures or the words to help them figure out what the book is about.
- **Game 1: Looking for Clues in Pictures**
  Hold up a picture of a person showing an obvious emotion (the black-and-white photo-cards from the Second Step program work well), or demonstrate an emotion yourself. Ask students to try to infer what the person (or you) is feeling. If you are demonstrating the emotion, make sure to use facial expressions and body language. Encourage students to use inferring words, such as "I think…", "Maybe…", "Perhaps…", "I'm inferring…" When someone guesses, ask, "What were the clues that helped you infer that?" Try to get students to be very specific. Repeat several times, inviting students to come up and demonstrate their own emotions for the class to guess. Give feedback like "Great! You inferred that!" and "Good inference!" as much as possible. Pass out Inferring from Pictures sheet (pages 120–121) and invite students to practice inferring from the pictures.

When modeling inferring with a picture book, don't forget to share the title page and/or dedication page. Although we tend to skip over these pages to get to the story, authors and illustrators often leave important clues there.

- **Game 2: Looking for Clues in the Text** (adapted from Harvey & Goudvis) Choose one student to come to the front of the class. Explain that you are going to tape a card with an emotion (e.g., *disappointed*) written on it to the student's back. The class will give clues to help the student determine what emotion it is. In order to give a clue, students need to think of a time when they actually felt that way, then phrase their clue like this: "I felt that way once when…" (e.g., "I felt that way once when I was hoping for something for my birthday, but I never got it"). The student at the front needs to listen to at least three clues before inferring the emotion. Invite other students to take turns with different emotions. End the lesson by generating an anchor chart for Inferring and post it in the classroom.

SAMPLE INFERRING ANCHOR CHART

Good Readers INFER!

When I infer, I…
- know that authors don't always write everything in the book
- fill in or add a "maybe" into the story
- use clues in the pictures and text plus my own thinking to help me infer

"Maybe…"
"I think…"
"Perhaps…"
"It could be…"
"It's because…"
"It might be…"

Lesson 2 (Teacher Directed): Inferring from Wordless Books

- Explain to students that some books are written with no words at all, but that good readers can look for clues in the pictures and infer the story.
- Choose a wordless picture book and flip through the pages quickly.

   There are no words at all in this story. This story is told through the pictures (illustrations). I'm going to model how I look carefully at the clues in the picture and then infer what is going on."

(Turn to page one.)

   On this page, there is no writing, but there is a lot going on in the picture. I see… (describe what you see). Even though the author didn't write any words down, I can infer a lot from this picture. I infer… (make some inferences using "I think" or "Maybe")

- Continue reading and modeling what you see and what you infer.
- Ask students to help: "Who can tell me what you see on this page?" "Who can infer what is happening?"
- Suggested books for this lesson are *The Farmer and the Clown* by Marla Frazee; *Pancakes for Breakfast* by Tomie DePaola; *The Red Book* or *Museum Trip* by Barbara Lehman. For older students, the wordless picture book *War* by Popov is exceptionally powerful, telling how wars are started and high the cost we pay

From wordless picture books *Sidewalk Flowers* by JonArno Lawson and *Wait* by Antoinette Portis, readers will infer a parallel message about paying attention to the world around you.

for them completely through illustrations, leaving the reader to infer the entire story. *Rose Blanche* by Christophe Gallaz is another powerful book depicting the Nazi invasion through the eyes of a young Jewish girl.

Lessons 3–5 (Teacher Directed/Group Practice): Inferring from Very Little Text

- Books that use very little text to tell their stories are excellent for modeling and practicing inferring. Explain to the students that some authors can write an entire story using only one or two words. Usually these authors are also the illustrators, so they use their illustrations to tell the story. A good reader needs to look for clues in the illustrations to infer what the author *didn't* write.
- Begin to model:

> Now there is only one word on this page and the word is "_____." But I can look carefully at the clues in the picture and use the word, the picture, and my own thinking to infer what is going on in the picture. I see… (point to a few things on the page) and so I'm inferring….

- Continue this with the first few pages of the book, describing what you see in front of you, then making some inferences.
- After modeling three or four pages, ask if there is someone who would like to model inferring for the next page. Continue reading, having different students model what they see and what they infer.
- Continue reading. Students share in partners what they see and what they infer.
- Writing extension: Have students choose one page of the book (you can photocopy a few pages for them to choose from). Pass out Talking Balloons and Thinking Bubbles (page 122) and invite students to fill in what they think the character is saying. Students can glue the bubbles on the photocopy (see sample below).
- Suggested Primary books for these lessons: *Hug* by Jez Alborough ("hug" is the only word in the book); *Oink!* by Karen J. Lammie; *A Splendid Friend, Indeed* by Suzanne Bloom; *Look!* By Jeff Mack; *Mama* by Jeanette Winter; *Uh-Oh!* by Shutta Crum.
- Suggested Intermediate books for these lessons: *Dude* by Christopher Aslan; *Yo! Yes!* by Chris Raschka; *No!* by David McPhail.

Pay attention to changes in text size and font. These are often clues left for the reader to help infer meaning.

While more applicable for slightly older students, there is a hilarious and very clever new series by Brett Wright: classic Shakespeare told entirely in text messages, status updates, and emojis! Students can infer the story through the text dialogue. Titles include: *YOLO Juliet*, *srsly Hamlet*, *A Midsummer Night #nofilter*, and *Macbeth #killingit*.

Grade 6 Sample

When using *Underground* by Shane Evans, the story of the Underground Railway with very sparse text, I give copies of only the text to students, with the title removed. In groups, they read the words and try to infer what the text is about. Some inferences students have come up with include escaping from jail, a sea turtle's journey, a plant growing, and going to school.

Lesson 6 (Independent Practice): Creating a Dialogue

The first time I did this lesson with a Gr. 5 class, I got a collection of raps—"Yo!" "Hey!" "Wuz up?" "Wuz happenin'"—but none of them told a story. The challenge in this activity is to plan the story ahead of time so you can leave enough clues for the reader to infer a story.

- Remind students that some authors don't write everything, but will leave clues in their illustrations and elements of type to help their readers infer meaning.
- After reading the book *Yo! Yes!* by Chris Raschka, have students create a dialogue between two characters, using the Inferring Dialogue template on page 123. The criteria are that the dialogue is no longer than six exchanges, and each character is allowed to say only one or two words per exchange.
- Students must provide clues for the reader to infer the meaning of the story, such as pictures or a change in text or font.
- Pairs of students can act out their dialogues for the class.
- Suggested books for this lesson: *Yo! Yes!* by Chris Raschka; *Look!* by Jeff Mack; *Hug!* By Jez Alborough.

Lesson 7 (Guided Practice): Inferring from Clues

- Remind students that sometimes authors intentionally leave clues for the reader throughout the book, providing information a little at a time to reveal a mystery at the end. Good readers will pay attention to the clues as they read and try to infer what the mystery is.
- Provide the students with the Inferring from Clues chart on page 124. Explain that you are going to read a story that gives clues but does not tell them right away about a mystery object.
- Begin by just reading the title: DO NOT show the students the cover or any illustrations. Using *Little Green* by Keith Baker, ask students to infer just from that title what or who Little Green might be. Have them draw a picture and write the sentence in the first box. In partners, they can share their Little Greens with each other.
- Tell students to listen carefully for clues in the story to see if their Little Green fits or not. After reading each page, ask them to draw and write what they infer from the clues now. Is their Little Green fitting into the clues or do they need to change their Little Green? What were the clues that made them change their minds?
- Finish reading the story and ask students to make their final inference of what Little Green is. Reveal the cover and reread the story, showing the illustrations. Have students complete the last box.
- Suggested books for this lesson: *Little Green* or *Who Is the Beast?* by Keith Baker; *Seven Blind Mice* by Ed Young (seven blind mice all feel different parts of an elephant, trying to determine what "the thing" is; students listen to the clues of each of the mice to try to infer what the mice are feeling); *Underground* by Shane Evans.

Lesson 8 (Independent Practice): Inferring with Comics

- Photocopy a comic strip and cut out each frame separately. Glue the frames onto a long strip of white paper, leaving a blank frame between each comic frame.
- Have the students fill in—with words or pictures—what they think happened between each frame.
- Another option for this lesson is to copy a page from a comic book and remove the dialogue. Students can infer what the conversation might be and add their own dialogue to the page.
- Suggested comics for this lesson: *Garfield, Calvin and Hobbes.*

Lesson 9 (Teacher Directed): Inferring from Illustrations: OWI

- From a picture book, select one illustration that "tells a story." Show this picture to the class using a document camera or by photocopying the page. Make sure no text is included. Pass out the OWI form (page 125)
- On chart paper, make three column headings: *What I Observe, What I Wonder, What I Infer.* Model to students how to complete the What I **O**bserve column by looking carefully for clues in the picture and writing down a description of only what you can see. After modeling two or three illustrations, ask students to participate and record their responses on the chart paper. Use the opportunity to point out that, when someone says "Maybe…" or "I think…," they are actually making an inference. Write their comments in the third column.
- Complete the What I **W**onder column by modeling your questions. Students can add their questions. Record their responses in the middle column.
- Complete the What I **I**nfer column by telling students that it is time for them to fill in what they think is going on in the picture. Model how an inference needs to begin with "I think…" or "Maybe…" to reinforce the notion that, when you make an inference, you are writing what you think based on your observation of the picture, not on what the author actually has written.

This lesson works very well with real photographs taken from newspapers or nonfiction texts. I often use it as a starting point for current events.

- Allow students time with a partner to share and compare their OWI pages.
- End the lesson by reading the picture book. Students will enjoy discovering where the single image came from and what the story is about.
- Suggested books for this lesson: *Tight Times* by Barbara Shook Hazen; *Queen of the Falls*, *The Mysteries of Harris Burdick*, or *The Sweetest Fig* by Chris Van Allsburg; *Tuesday* or *June 29, 1999* by David Wiesner; *Tough Boris* by Mem Fox.

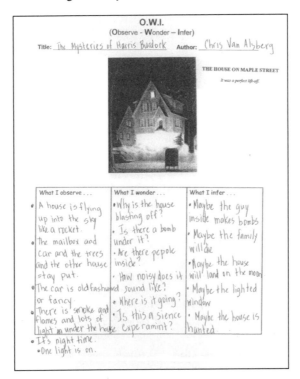

The portfolio edition of Chris Van Allsburg's *Mysteries of Harris Burdick* provides large illustrations on separate cards and lends itself perfectly to a group OWI. Many years after this highly successful book was published in 1984, Chris Van Allsburg invited renowned authors to write stories about each of the illustrations from the book and published *The Chronicles of Harris Burdick*. While the content of a few of the stories is for a slightly older audience, there are several worth reading aloud to your students after they have explored the illustrations through OWI.

Lesson 10 (Independent Practice): 3, 2, 1—OWI!

- Choose an illustration from a book suggested for Lesson 9. Copy it into the box at the top of the OWI sheet on page 125. Or you can display it on your computer or interactive whiteboard screen and use the half-page template for 3, 2, 1—OWI! on page 126.
- Students complete the chart independently, writing three observations, two questions, and one inference they make from studying the image. Have student share their inferences with partners.

3, 2, 1 stands for: 3 observations, 2 questions, 1 inference.

- Once the students have shared their OWI with a partner, read the story or portion of the story. Remind students that it's not about getting the "right" answer but about being able to justify your inference.

- Repeat this lesson, inviting students to find their own OWI illustration to use and to exchange their OWI pictures with a partner.

Lesson 11 (Teacher Directed): OWI with Text

- Review the game Looking for Clues in the Text on page 112. Remind students the secret of inferring: Not all authors tell you everything, and it's up to you, the reader, to look carefully at what the author did tell you, and then fill in what they didn't tell you.
- On chart paper, make three columns: *Observe, Wonder,* and *Infer.* Explain that you will be practicing the OWI again, but this time with a story. Explain that the OWI activity works the same way as before, except that they will be reading words instead of looking at pictures.
- Choose a book from the Infer Books. Read the first page. In the first column, write down something you know from the first page because the author actually wrote it. Model how you wonder something about that fact; write the question in the second column. Model an inference that answers the question—one that begins with "I think..." or "Maybe..."—and write it in the last column. Draw a line under your writing to indicate a new page.
- Continue modeling this with two or three more pages. Then ask students to participate. Read a page and ask, "What do you know because the author actually wrote it?" Record their responses. Then move to the second column and ask, "What are you wondering about that?" Finally, record their answers to "What can you infer?" in the third column.
- Suggested books for this lesson: Willy books or *Voices in the Park* by Anthony Browne; *Fox* by Margaret Wild; *The Promise* by Nicola Davies.
- Explain that, when readers infer, they actually do an OWI inside their heads. The activity shows thinking in slow motion and made visible for them. Eventually, the goal is that they will move from text to inference automatically without having to write it down.

Lesson 12 (Independent Practice): Inferring from Text

- Students choose their own books. Supply students with OWI with Text chart on page 127.
- Students complete chart and share their inferences with the class or with partners.

This way of reading, stopping, thinking, wondering, and inferring on paper is time-consuming and not something I make students do every time they read. It is important to point out to students that what you are doing in this activity is *slowing down their thinking* so that they can see what an inference feels like and where it comes from. In real-life reading experiences, inferences occur inside our heads and sometimes they happen so quickly, we hardly notice them. Good readers, however, pay just as much attention to what authors *didn't* write as to what they *did* write.

Lesson 13: Reflective Journal

Have students record their thoughts about this new strategy and what they've learned about inferring. *How has inferring while you read helped you to understand the story better? Show me or tell me about your thinking.*

Inferring with Older Students

For Infer texts to use with older students, see page 119. A great way to practice inferring is to give older students *Aesop's Fables*, but with the morals removed. Read the story and have students infer the moral. It might be necessary to explain what a moral is and to brainstorm common morals prior to reading.

After introducing, modeling, and practicing the strategy of inferring, use the concept to teach students the literary device of direct and indirect characterization. Explain the difference between direct characterization (information about character provided directly from author) and indirect characterization (information reader infers based on character's actions, words, and thoughts). After reading a short story, create a characterization chart with two columns: *Direct* and *Indirect*. Invite students to describe a character by putting specific examples from the book in the Direct column and Recording characteristics they infer in the Indirect column.

Assessing Inferencing

NY = Not Yet Meeting Grade Level Expectations
M = Meeting Expectations at a Minimal Level
FM = Fully Meeting Grade Expectations
EX = Exceeding Expectations

ASSESSMENT RUBRIC FOR INFERRING

Making Inferences	NY	M	FM	EX
Is able to make simple inferences from a picture or photo.				
Uses background knowledge and experiences, plus the clues from the text, to support his/her inference.				
Can tell at least two things that are not written in the text or shown in the picture and give reasons for them with little or no support.				
Uses the language of thinking without prompting: "Maybe…" "I think…" "It could be…" "It's because…" "Perhaps…" "It means that…"				

Infer Books

P = Primary
I = Intermediate

Choose from the following books to create a collection of Infer books for your classroom. Try to include some wordless books, some books with very little text, and some books with longer text to scaffold their understanding of the strategy.

WORDLESS PICTURE BOOKS

Baker, Jeannie. *Mirror* (I)
Baker, Jeannie. *Window* (I)
Banyai, Istvan. *Zoom* (P, I)
Becker, Aaron. *Journey* (P, I)
Boyd, Lizi. *Inside Outside* (P)
Day, Alexandra. *Carl Goes Shopping* (P)
Day, Alexandra. *Good Dog, Carl* (P)
DePaola, Tomie. *Pancakes for Breakfast.* (P)
Frazee, Marlee. *The Farmer and the Clown* (P, I)
Gallaz, Christophe. *Rose Blanche* (I)

Idle, Molly. *Flora and the Flamingo* (P, I)
Idle, Molly. *Flora and the Penguin* (P, I)
Kim, Patti. *Here I Am* (P)
Lawson, JonArno. *Sidewalk Flowers* (P, I)
Lee, JiHyeon. *Pool* (P, I)
Lee, Suzy. *Wave* (P, I)
Lehman, Barbara. *Museum Trip* (P, I)
Lehman, Barbara. *The Red Book* (P, I)
Mack, Jeff. *Look!* (P)
Miyares, Daniel. *Float* (P)
Pett, Mark. *The Boy and the Airplane* (P, I)

Pett, Mark. *The Girl and the Bicycle* (P, I)
Pinkney, Jerry. *The Lion and the Mouse* (P, I)
Popov. *Why?* (I)
Portis, Antoinette. *Wait* (P, I)
Princesse Camcam. *Fox's Garden* (P, I)
Raschka, Chris. *A Ball for Daisy* (P)
Staake, Bob. *Bluebird* (I)
Tan, Shaun. *Rules of Summer* (I)
Tan, Shaun. *The Arrival* (I)
Thomson, Bill. *Chalk* (I)
Thomson, Bill. *Fossil* (I)
Van Hout, Mies. *Happy* (P)
Van Ommen, Sylvia. *The Surprise* (P)
Wiesner, David. *Flotsam* (P, I)
Wiesner, David. *Mr. Wuffles!* (P, I)
Young, Ed. *Seven Blind Mice* (P, I)

BOOKS WITH VERY LITTLE TEXT

Alborough, Jez. *Hug.* (P)
Alexander, Jed. *(Mostly) Wordless* (P)
Aslan, Christopher. *Dude* (I)
Baker, Keith. *Little Green* (P, I)
Baker, Keith. *Who Is the Beast?* (P, I)
Bloom, Suzanne. *A Splendid Friend, Indeed* (P)
Crum, Shutta. *Uh-Oh!* (P)
Evans, Shane. *Underground* (I)
Haughton, Chris. *Shh! We Have a Plan* (P)
Hest, Amy. *The Reader* (P, I)
Klassen, Jon. *I Want My Hat Back* (P)
Klassen, Jon. *This Is Not My Hat* (P)
Raschka, Chris. *Yo! Yes!* (I)
Springman, I.C. *More* (P, I)
Tan, Shaun. *The Red Tree* (I)

Van Allsburg, Chris. *The Mysteries of Harris Burdick* (I)
Wiesner, David. *Tuesday* (I)
Zullo, Germano. *Little Bird* (P, I)

INFERRING BOOKS

Bottner, Barbara. *Bootsie Barker Bites* (P, I)
Browne, Anthony. *Changes* (P, I)
Browne, Anthony. *Piggybook* (P, I)
Browne, Anthony. *Voices in the Park.* (I)
Browne, Anthony. *Willy the Wimp.* (P, I)
Browne, Anthony. *Willy the Wizard.* (P, I)
Browne, Anthony. *Zoo* (I)
Davies, Jim. Any *Garfield* book (P, I)
Fox, Mem. *Tough Boris* (P, I)
Hazen, Barbara Shook. *Tight Times* (P, I)
Lobel, Arnold. *Fables* (I)
Marshall, James. *George and Martha* (I)
Van Allsburg, Chris. *The Garden of Abdul Gasazi* (I)
Van Allsburg, Chris. *Just a Dream* (I)
Van Allsburg, Chris. *The Stranger* (I)
Van Allsburg, Chris. *The Sweetest Fig* (I)
Willems, Mo. *Knuffle Bunny* (P)

INFER TEXTS FOR OLDER STUDENTS (GRADES 8–12)

Aesop, Fables (various versions)
Browne, Anthony. *Voices in the Park* (picture book)
Bunting, Eve. *Terrible Things: An Allegory of the Holocaust* (picture book)
Dahl, Roald. "The Visitor" (short story)
Dahl, Roald. "Dip in the Pool" (short story)
Pentecost, Hugh. "A Kind of Murder" (short story)
Wilson, Budge. "The Metaphor" (short story)

Inferring from Pictures

Name: _____ Date: _____

	I'm inferring they are feeling _____ Clue #1: _____ Clue #2: _____ Maybe... _____ _____ _____
	I'm inferring he is feeling _____ Clue #1: _____ Clue #2: _____ Maybe... _____ _____ _____
	I'm inferring she is feeling _____ Clue #1: _____ Clue #2: _____ Maybe... _____ _____ _____

Pembroke Publishers © 2015 *Reading Power, Revised and Expanded* by Adrienne Gear ISBN 978-1-55138-310-1

Inferring from Pictures (continued)

	I'm inferring he is feeling _____ Clue #1: _____ Clue #2: _____ Maybe… _____ _____ _____
	I'm inferring he is feeling _____ Clue #1: _____ Clue #2: _____ Maybe… _____ _____ _____
	I'm inferring he is feeling _____ Clue #1: _____ Clue #2: _____ Maybe… _____ _____ _____

Pembroke Publishers © 2015 *Reading Power, Revised and Expanded* by Adrienne Gear ISBN 978-1-55138-310-1

Talking Balloons and Thinking Bubbles

Name: _____   Date: _____

Title: _____

Inferring Dialogue

Name: _____   Date: _____

Create a dialogue between two people. Each person is only allowed to say ONE or TWO words each time they speak. Use speaking and thinking bubbles. Leave clues in the pictures and in the font size to help the reader infer what the characters are saying.

<table>
<tr><td></td><td></td></tr>
</table>

_____   _____

<table>
<tr><td></td><td></td></tr>
<tr><td></td><td></td></tr>
<tr><td></td><td></td></tr>
<tr><td></td><td></td></tr>
</table>

Pembroke Publishers © 2015 *Reading Power, Revised and Expanded* by Adrienne Gear ISBN 978-1-55138-310-1

Inferring from Clues

Name: _____   Date: _____

Title: _____   Author: _____

I think _____

Now, I think_____

Now, I know _____

Pembroke Publishers © 2015 *Reading Power, Revised and Expanded* by Adrienne Gear ISBN 978-1-55138-310-1

OWI

Name: _____   Date: _____

Place photo or illustration here

What I **O**bserve	What I **W**onder	What I **I**nfer
_____	_____	_____
_____	_____	_____
_____	_____	_____
_____	_____	_____
_____	_____	_____
_____	_____	_____
_____	_____	_____
_____	_____	_____
_____	_____	_____
_____	_____	_____

Pembroke Publishers © 2015 *Reading Power, Revised and Expanded* by Adrienne Gear ISBN 978-1-55138-310-1

3, 2, 1—OWl!

Name: _____   Date: _____

Observe	Wonder	Infer
1. _____ _____ 2. _____ _____ 3. _____ _____	1. _____ _____ 2. _____ _____ _____	_____ _____ _____ _____ _____

Name: _____   Date: _____

Observe	Wonder	Infer
1. _____ _____ 2. _____ _____ 3. _____ _____	1. _____ _____ 2. _____ _____ _____	_____ _____ _____ _____ _____

Pembroke Publishers © 2015 *Reading Power, Revised and Expanded* by Adrienne Gear ISBN 978-1-55138-310-1

OWI with Text

Name: _____ Date: _____

Good readers **infer** when they read. Authors sometimes don't tell us everything. Readers need to become **book detectives**. They need to look for the clues and think about the *maybe*…s.

OBSERVE What the author wrote: facts from the text	WONDER A question you have: what did the author NOT tell you?	INFER Add your *maybe*…: what are you **thinking** about?

Pembroke Publishers © 2015 *Reading Power, Revised and Expanded* by Adrienne Gear ISBN 978-1-55138-310-1

7 The Power to Transform

Transform Chant

Synthesize! Synthesize!
Transform your thinking
Let's synthesize!
Read a little, think a lot
Everyone tries
To make new meaning—
Let's synthesize!

Synthesize! Synthesize!
Transform your thinking
Let's synthesize!
Thinkin' starts a-changin'
Ideas start rearrangin'
You'll be surprised
Just how easy
You can synthesize!

Transform Song
(to the tune of "Row, Row, Row Your Boat)

When you read a book
Thoughts can sometimes change.
Some ideas inside your head
Will sometimes rearrange.

What you thought before
Might not be the same
As what you might be thinking now.
How has your thinking changed?

Reading's not just in the book.
It's more than just the facts.
A book can sometimes change the way
You think, or feel, or act!

✳ ✳ ✳

"Think of those times when you've read prose or poetry that is presented in such a way that you have a fleeting sense of being startled by beauty or insight, by a glimpse into someone's soul. All of a sudden everything seems to fit together or at the very least to have some meaning for a moment."
—Annie Dillard, *Bird by Bird*

When I first read the book *Miss Rumphius* by Barbara Cooney, I was transformed. I can honestly say that I changed the way I lived my life because of that book. In the story, young Alice tells her grandfather, whom she adores, that she wants to be just like him when she grows up: "When I grow up, Grandfather, I too will travel to far away places and then I will come home and live by the sea." But her grandfather reminds her that there is a third thing that she must do in her life: "to make the world more beautiful." In the story, Alice makes the world more aesthetically beautiful by scattering lupine seeds all around her village. For me, finding my own "third thing" became an important question: What was I going to do in my life to make the world a better place: what was I going to do to make a difference? I followed in Alice's footsteps and "traveled to far away places" when I taught in Japan for three years. Then I returned to Vancouver to "live by the sea." And my third thing? Well, I still don't know what my third thing is. And while I may not remember the names of the far-away places Alice traveled to or what color the lupines were that she planted, what I do remember from that story and what mattered to me most was the possibility of a "third thing"—an awareness and an openness to the possibility, and perhaps responsibility, to make the world a better place. This was my transformation. This was my mind sifting through the details of the story and connecting them to a meaningful whole—to what mattered most to me.

During the years I've spent teaching Reading Power to children and teachers, the strategies continue to evolve. This has been especially true of this last, and perhaps most complex, strategy. The word *transform* has its roots in the strategy of synthesizing. In the early stages of developing Reading Power, I lacked the courage to attempt to integrate the power to Synthesize because of my uncertainty of what it would look like in the classroom. I initially changed the name of the power to Transform because I believed it to be a word more familiar to children. Now, as the term "synthesize" is being used in upper-intermediate and high-school classrooms, I realize that teaching synthesizing strategies is a natural part of teaching the Transform power. The word *transform* refers to the notion that certain books can change the way we think about ourselves, about others, or about the world. Like synthesizing, it is an openness, a willingness, an awareness to sort through the details of a story and focus on those pieces that matter most to us. When we synthesize, we reorganize a story in terms of our own lives and experiences. Synthesizing or transforming combines and builds upon all four previous reading powers: it is the accumulation of the connections, the questions, the inferences, and the visual imagery combined to create the new or possible revision of a previous thought.

Some of my colleagues attended the International Reading Association's annual conference in Chicago several years ago. There was interesting talk about some of the sessions they attended on recent trends and directions of comprehension instruction, a commonality of messages from leading educators in the field that I feel is worth noting. The overall message was that, if we continue to focus on comprehension strategies rather than critical thinking, we are in danger of creating a dilemma we did not intend. If we teach comprehension strategies in isolation, our students might indeed learn to mirror what good readers do; however, if we isolate strategies solely for the purpose of comprehension, we are missing an important piece of critical thought. We need to be mindful of this, to continue to bring our students back to the big picture—the integrated whole, the structure and framework of critical thought. While we celebrate when our students begin to make connections or visualize, we cannot stop there. Moral ethic

"The good news is that comprehension instruction has become a long overdue reading focus. The bad news is that comprehension strategies and exercises often dominate comprehension instruction. Students are spending massive amounts of time learning and practicing these strategies, often without knowing how to apply them or not understanding how they fit into the big picture of reading."
—Regie Routman, *Reading Essentials*

"The most rigorous reading is to find what those words on that page mean in our own lives."
—Kylene Beers, *Notice & Note: Strategies for Close Reading*

is created when we provide our students with opportunities to develop thinking, reasoning, and judgment skills through complex, real-world issues. Comprehension instruction must set the groundwork for instruction in critical thinking.

In terms of Reading Power, it is imperative that we not rest on our laurels when our students have mastered connecting, but that we continue teaching through the other strategies. Teaching Transform and the moral issues introduced through specific books can be the first step towards laying the groundwork for critical thinking; it can lead our students towards a bigger context, providing them with a broader avenue to show their thinking. Reading deeply is not just being able to say what the book is about or what connection we made to a particular part. Reading deeply is being able to understand our own lives a little better through the pages of the book.

I remember very clearly being taught in high school how to summarize: pulling out key ideas and rewriting them into a short paragraph "in my own words." These short paragraphs, as I recall, were to contain the key ideas of the piece, but my own thoughts or opinions were never to be included. Marks were taken off, in fact, if anything other than what was in the passage was included. While summarizing is the first step in synthesizing, it is certainly only a part of it. I now see summarizing as 2D (two-dimensional) reading—information from the text made smaller. But synthesizing can be interpreted as 3D reading—key points from the text, plus the reader's thinking to create a new thought. When we synthesize, we add another layer to our reading: that other layer is our thinking, our background knowledge, and our experiences. This was the layer that I was discouraged from including in my summary paragraphs in high school, but the layer I now cannot imagine omitting from my teaching.

When readers are transformed by what they read...

- they understand that books have the ability to change the way we think about ourselves and our world.
- they are touched in some way by the words on the page, the thoughts in their heads, and the feelings in their hearts.
- they are introduced to books that deal with thought-provoking issues: war, conservation, perseverance, bullying, creativity, making a difference.
- they learn to look beyond the pages of the text towards the implications and effects the book may have on their own lives.
- they are challenged by change.
- they understand that transformation takes place over time, and that reading a particular book plants seeds that might one day make a difference to the way they live or view the world.
- they know that a story has the power to change them, because their brains have the power to store away facts, stories, questions, and feelings that will shape their lives.
- they learn to look for the things in a book that matter most to them.
- they ask themselves, "What difference has this book made to me?" or "Has anything in me changed because of this book?"
- they are learning that being able to identify what matters to them is the beginning of being shaped by the world around them.

"A good book reaches deep inside and shakes the heart awake."
—Jean Little

In order to teach this complex strategy to children, we turn, once again, to literature as a starting point. There are, as with all the reading powers, particular books that lend themselves well to this strategy. These are the books that offer readers opportunities to find the meaningful pieces hidden amongst the details of the story. (Often a few tissue boxes are required for reading!) These messages are sometimes very obvious, as in *Ordinary Mary's Extraordinary Deed* by Emily Pearson, and sometimes less so, as in *The Dot* by Peter H. Reynolds or *Mr. Peabody's Apples* by Madonna.

While some may see transforming as a complex strategy, I have noticed how naturally children begin to interpret and infuse the details of their own lives with the highlights of the text to find embedded meaning. I was teaching a Transform lesson in a Grade 4 classroom and modeled my thinking using the book *Ish* by Peter H. Reynolds, the story of a young artist whose creativity is suddenly halted by the stinging words of his older brother, but who is helped to regain his confidence by his sister's view of his art. After reading and filling out the Reading Voice/Thinking Voice chart (see page 148), I shared with the students my synthesis for the story:

> I think this story is about how sometimes what we say and what we do can have a tremendous impact on other people. I remember feeling very insecure about myself in elementary school because people used to make fun of me because I wore dresses. Their cruel words, just like those of Raymond's brother, affected me. This book reminded me how powerful words can be—both in a negative way and in a positive way.

I then reminded the students that, just as all of us are different, our syntheses of a story can also differ. I asked if anyone had a different synthesis that they would like to share. One boy put up his hand and said, "I think the book is about how sometimes you need to go to a bad place before you can get to the good place. The thing I'm taking from this book is that even when I feel terrible and think my life sucks, it's gonna get better eventually."

I was overwhelmed. "Wow," I choked, holding back tears. "You have synthesized far beyond what I did and you have helped make this book even more meaningful for me. Thank you." If I ever had doubts about children being capable of synthesizing, that nine-year-old boy put them to rest.

In my position as workshop presenter, it is important for me to give teachers a clear picture of a strategy so that they not only understand it, but also can easily apply it to their practice. The Transform strategy proved challenging for me in this respect because of the complexity of the idea of synthesis. Stephanie Harvey states, "synthesizing involves combining new information with existing knowledge to form an original idea, a new line of thinking, or a new creation" (1998, p. 137). However, I needed more than a definition if I was to be teaching teachers to teach students what the strategy really looks like. For concrete examples, I found it helpful to refer to two everyday words that share the same root—a synthesizer and synthetic fabric. A synthesizer combines different musical instruments to create a new sound. Synthetic fabric combines different materials to create a new material. A good reader combines information from text with background knowledge to create a new idea or thought. This new thought then becomes integrated into their own thinking.

To explain this concept to children, however, I like to use something concrete or visual (as I do with many of my lessons). A Transformer toy is something most

Passing out piles of LEGO pieces to groups and inviting them to transform their pieces into something new provides a concrete visual for the concept. Noticing that each group arranges their pieces in different ways helps to show that there is no "correct" way to synthesize text. Inviting them to deconstruct, then reconstruct, their pieces in a different way illustrates that our thinking is constantly changing and rearranging when we read.

children will be able to connect to and one that I find helpful in explaining the concept clearly. I will warn you that, speaking from personal experience, unless you know how to actually transform the toy from a robot into a vehicle, do not attempt this with a real toy, or your lesson will become about the toy and not about the concept! Using a photograph or just a simple drawing of a transformer toy works just as well.

New Thinking about Transform

While most teachers who are using Reading Power and teaching their students the different strategies feel comfortable with the previous four reading powers (Connect, Visualize, Question, and Infer), I have heard from many that they get stuck when it comes to the strategy of Transform. Some admit to skipping it altogether, while others confess to not really having a clear picture themselves about what it is and how to teach it. I have spent time revising my lessons to try to achieve some clarity for teachers, so that they don't feel as stuck with this final strategy. Specifically, I have introduced the concept of taking stock of our thinking, before and after reading. In this respect, the ability to transform becomes more concrete, and students can better understand how a story can change the way we think about something. It is my hope that the lesson One Word Activity on page 134 will help those of you who might have felt stymied by this strategy, so you can help your students understand the concept more clearly.

I have often been asked by teachers, "How do you explain Transform to kids?" Another way I have fine-tuned my thinking about this strategy is to develop some key words, phrases, and questions to use in teaching and talking about Transform with my students. Language plays a pivotal role in helping students understand the strategy more clearly. The Language of Transform chart on page 143 is a collection of key words, clear phrases, and prompting questions, specifically for teachers to use when teaching or explaining this strategy. It is intended as a teacher reference, a cheat sheet of sorts, and might provide you with clarity so that, in turn, you can be clearer with your students.

Sequential Lessons for Transform

Lesson 1 (Teacher Directed): Introducing the Power of Transforming

- Place the Transform brain piece into the Reading Power Model and tell students that you are going to be learning a new reading power called *Transform*.
- Explain that transformation is something that happens when we read and something in the book "sticks" and becomes part of our thinking.
- Show a picture or draw a picture of a Transformer toy. Ask students if they have seen one or know what it is? (Most will put up their hands.)
- Ask students the following questions about the transformer toy:

     What is it? (a Transformer toy)
     What does it do? (It transforms or changes from a robot into a vehicle.)
     How does it change? Remote control? Voice activation?
     (Move pieces around)

- Write the words *rearrange*, *reorganize*, and *reconstruct* on the board. Ask students what they notice about those words. (They all start with *re–*)

"In order to construct any kind of meaning in our literacy learning and our life learning, we must find ways to cull and prune the details with which we are bombarded. We must *reorganize* and *create our own explanations* for what we are learning, our own definitions of our lives at any particular juncture."
—Ellin Keene & Susan Zimmerman, *Mosaic of Thought*

- Explain that "re–" means "again"—in other words, when you rearrange or reorganize the pieces of the Transformer, you are moving them around again.
- Ask a last question:

  Once it's been transformed, is it a new toy or the same toy? (This question will be one to debate, as it could be seen as both.)

- Ask students if they would all agree that once the toy has been transformed, it's still the same toy, only now it looks different. (Write *still the same but look different* on board or interactive whiteboard.

What is a TRANSFORMER?

A toy that starts out as a robot and then changes into a car.

How does it change?

You move the pieces around: rearrange, reorganize them.

Once it's been transformed, is it a different toy?

No, it's the same toy, only now it looks different.

- Tell students you don't really want to talk about Transformer toys but that the example you just shared has a connection to reading. Older students might be able to make the connection.

  We all have ideas and thoughts in our heads before we start reading. Sometimes while we're reading, our thoughts get reorganized and rearranged. When we've finished reading, our thoughts might look a little different because of what we just read. Our brain might be saying, "Hmmmm, I had never thought about it that way before." All of a sudden, the idea from the book has mixed with the ideas in our head and now our thinking looks different. When this happens, we call it "synthesizing" or "transformed thinking." Sometimes a book can change the way we think about something. When that happens, I call it a "thinking adjustment"!

- Create a class Transform Anchor Chart to display in the classroom.

SAMPLE TRANSFORM ANCHOR CHART

Good Readers Are Transformed!

- Sometimes a book can change or rearrange the way we think about ourselves, others, or the world!
- Sometimes it's a thought we already had, only now it looks different.

ideas from the book + our thinking = transformed thought

Now I'm thinking...
This makes me think of...
I used to think...but now I'm thinking...
I now understand that...
I always knew that... but now I understand....
Hmmmm...I had never thought of it that way before...

Lesson 2 (Teacher Directed): A Change in Thinking

Cybelle Young's extraordinary book *Some Things I've Lost* provides concrete illustrations for the concept of transformation by showing numerous misplaced everyday objects transformed into imaginative, mysterious sea creatures.

- Spend time reviewing the concept of Transform or "a change in thinking." Describe how reading can change the way we think about something and help us create a new way of thinking about something. The ideas from a book plus our own thoughts equal Transform.
- Prepare and model how a book that has made an impact on you has changed your thinking.
- After you have finished reading, model a synthesis of the theme or message of the story (see box below).

Transformed Thinking: *Miss Rumphius* by Barbara Cooney

After I finish reading this story, my thinking doesn't stop. This story has really changed my thinking a lot. In the book, Miss Rumphius made the world more beautiful by planting lupine seeds all over town. The important thing that I took from that book is that one person can make a big difference in the world. Now I'm wondering about what I can do that will make a difference in the world. I may not plant lupine seeds but I know that I really want to try to do something to make a difference. If I had never read this book, I may not have had this thought. My thinking has changed because of this book. That is what Transform is.

- Suggested books to use to model "a change in thinking": *Miss Rumphius* by Barbara Cooney (making a difference); *Yard Sale* by Eve Bunting (meaning of home); *Each Kindness* by Jacqueline Woodson (bullying); *Ordinary Mary's Extraordinary Deed* by Emily Pearson (random acts of kindness); *Mr. Peabody's Apples* by Madonna (spreading false rumors); *Last Stop on Market Street* by Matt de la Pena (paying attention); *Nora the Mind Reader* by Orit Gidali (what people say is not always what they mean).

Lesson 3 (Teacher Directed/ Student Participation): One Word Activity

"I think a writer's job is to provoke questions. I like to think that if someone's read a book of mine, they've had—I don't know what—the literary equivalent of a shower. Something that would start them thinking in a slightly different way, perhaps. That's what I think writers are for."
—Doris Lessing

One of the challenges when teaching the strategy of Transform is articulating how our thinking has changed. I developed this before-and-after-thinking lesson as a way to help students see how their thinking can shift because of something that they read. While it may seem a bit manipulative, with the right picture book it successfully demonstrates in a very concrete way how thinking changes.

- Begin the lesson:

Sometimes a book can change the way we think about something. We call this the power to *transform*. Sometimes authors want to share an important message with us. Other times, an author might want us to think about something in a different way, and so gives us a little thinking nudge. Sometimes, after I read a story, I wish that the author had written me a special message at the back of the book.

(Turn to the back page and pretend to read)

"Dear (teacher's name): After you have finished reading this book, these are the thoughts that I would like you to take away with you…. Here is the important message that I want you to think about…."

(Turn the book to show the blank page)

The author didn't actually write a special message to me. But as a good reader, I know that it's important to spend some time thinking about the book after I finish reading. I want to think to myself, *What part of this story "sticks"?* Remember that good readers know that just because the story stops, their thinking doesn't!

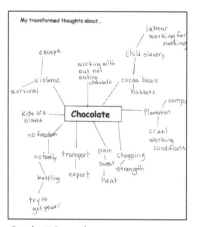

Grade 7 Sample

- Before reading a picture book to the class, read through and chose one word that, for you, represents the main message or theme from the story. (See Suggested Words and Corresponding Books below.)
- Explain to the class that you are going to be reading a book that may help them experience a change in their thinking.
- Write the one word on the board and tell students you will be reading a story to them that is connected to the word. Before you read, you want them to take stock of their thinking, or think about what thoughts or connections they already have about the word.
- Have students discuss the word in partners or small groups, either recording on a web (see One Word Activity: Part 1 template on page 144) or just talking. Discuss and make a class web.
- Tell students to pay close attention to their thinking as you read and notice if their thinking changes.
- Read the book to the class.
- After reading the story, invite students to revisit their thinking: *What are you thinking about now that you hadn't thought about before you read (or heard) the story?*
- Record their new thinking on a new web (Use One Word Activity: Part 2 template on page 145). Compare the two webs and discuss what students notice. Explain that sometimes reading a book can change the way we think about something. Once this happens, it is hard to go back to thinking about things in quite the same way as before.
- The next lesson/day, repeat the One Word Activity with another book. Students can work individually or in groups to create their webs.

I use this lesson to launch my literature circles. Before each group receives their novels, I give them one word connected to their novel and invite them to brainstorm in groups. After the novel is finished several weeks later, we revisit the word and students record their new thinking.

SUGGESTED WORDS AND CORRESPONDING BOOKS

words	Rozler, Lora. *Words* (I)
present	DiOrio, Rana. *What Does it Mean to Be Present?* (P, I)
green	DiOrio, Rana. *What Does it Mean to Be Green?* (P, I)
understanding	Gidali, Orit. *Nora the Mind Reader* (P)
kindness	Pearson, Emily. *Ordinary Mary's Extraordinary Deed* (P, I)
gossip	Madonna. *Mr. Peabody's Apples* (I) Keller, Holly. *Help! A Story of Friendship* (P)
dark	Snicket, Lemony. *The Dark* (P)
best	Cousins, Lucy. *I'm the Best!* (P)
invisible	Ludwig, Trudy. *The Invisible Boy* (P, I)

peace	Rudunsky, Vladimir. *What Does Peace Feel Like?* (P)
idea	Yamada, Kobi. *What Do You Do With an Idea?* (P, I)
zoo	Johnson, Mariana Ruiz. *I Know a Bear* (P)
jacket	Hall, Kirsten. *The Jacket* (P, I)
home	Bunting, Eve. *Yard Sale* (P, I)
footprint	Handy, Femida. *Sandy's Incredible Shrinking Footprint* (P, I)
pretty	Denomme, Margot. *Mommy, Am I Pretty?* (P)
breathe	Magoon, Scott. *Breathe* (P)
bully	Roberts, Justin. *The Smallest Girl in the Smallest Grade* (P)
trouble	Heide, Florence Parry. *Sami and the Time of the Troubles* (I)

Lessons 4–5 (Teacher Directed): Finding the Important Message

This lesson provides a stepping stone for students to begin to notice what matters in a story by reading a book with a very obvious message—making a difference

- Tell students you will read a book to them, and that you are going to see how this book has transformed (changed) their thinking. Remind them that transforming, or synthesizing, is paying attention to your thinking while you read and then finding what matters to you in the story.
- Choose a book in which the important message is how we can make a difference. Read aloud. Then have students find a partner and discuss: *How did the character in this story make a difference in the world? How might this story change your thinking? What could you do to make a difference?*
- Come together as a class to share. Have students complete the Making a Difference sheet on page 146.
- Suggested books for this lesson: *Ordinary Mary's Extraordinary Deed* by Emily Pearson; *The Teddy Bear* by David McPhail; *Miss Rumphius* by Barbara Cooney; *Those Shoes* by Maribeth Boelts; *Extra Yarn* by Mac Barnett; *How Full is Your Bucket?* by Tom Rath; *Butterfly Garden* by Elly MacKay.

Several months ago I received a message on my Facebook page from Christine Blessin, a Grade 3 teacher in Chilliwack, B.C., who had used this lesson and the Emily Pearson book to inspire her class to do random acts of kindness in the community. One little boy in her class was so inspired, he went above and beyond and raised a large sum of money by making and selling bracelets. He donated the money he made to Canuck Place, the hospital where his twin brother receives treatment for a rare genetic disorder.

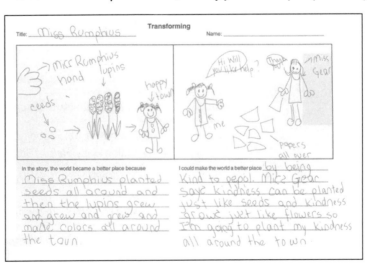

Transforming Our Thinking

First Day Jitters

My first thoughts......

Sara is a new girl and she feels nurvus about going to a new school and her dad is trying to get her to go anyways.

On second thought........ Surprise! Surprise!
Sara is not the student. She is the teacher! What a shock that was!

My transformed thought.........
Well I guess it's like this Grown-ups get nurvus to.

Grade 3 Sample

Lessons 6–7 (Teacher Directed/Student Participation): Thinking Changes as We Read

- Explain to students that sometimes when we start a book, we have ideas or thoughts about what the book is about, but while we read our thinking changes. At the end of the story, our thinking might be completely different from when we first started to read.
- Choose a book; see suggestions below. Books that have unexpected or surprise endings work well for this lesson. Pass out Noticing How My Thinking Changes (page 147).
- Read the first few pages of the book. Stop and have students fill in the first box. Invite students to share their ideas with the class or in partners.
- Continue reading through the rest of the story. Have students fill out the middle box on the sheet, and share with partners.
- Explain how the last box is similar to the work they have been doing in previous lessons: *What from this story is your "new thought"* (an idea or thought that you have now but might not have had before you heard this story)?
- Suggested books for this lesson: *Oi! Get Off Our Train* by John Burningham; *First Day Jitters* by Julie Danneberg; *Where Once There Was a Wood* by Denise Fleming; *Red: A Crayon's Story* by Michael Hall; *Each Kindness* by Jacqueline Woodson; "The Composition" by Antonio Skarmeta; *I Know A Bear* by Mariana Ruiz Johnson.

Lesson 8 (Teacher Directed): Looking for What Matters Most

- Choose a book that can be modeled as having an important message or impact on your life; i.e., a book with which you can model your transformed thought.
- Create a chart based on the Reading Voice/Thinking Voice template on page 148. On one side, you are going to write a short summary of what has happened up to a certain place in the story. On the other side, you are going to record your thinking voice.
- Begin to read aloud and stop after every few pages, recording your reading voice (summary) and your thinking voice on the chart paper.
- Try to model short summaries on the left and longer responses on the right. Draw students' attention to this:

  I notice that my summary is quite short and that's okay. In fact, I'm not as interested in this side, because it's basically retelling what I've already read. What I am more interested in is the right side, because this is the window into a reader's thinking. This is what's going to tell me how well you understand your thinking and are using your reading powers. So I'm going to be looking for lots of writing on this side of the page, when you are working on this on your own.

- Model your synthesis of the book:

  After reading and thinking about this book, I now want to add these two columns together and look at my new thoughts. What mattered most to me in this story? What part is going to stick with me long after I put the book away?"

  Remind students that, because we are all different, what matters to one person may be different from what matters to another.

- Suggested books for this lesson: *Miss Rumphius* by Barbara Cooney (making a difference); *Nana in the City* by Lauren Castillo (courage, taking risks); *Yard Sale* by Eve Bunting (true meaning of home); *Last Stop on Market Street* by Matt de la Pena (noticing, paying attention); *The Gift of Nothing* by Patrick McDonnell (the gift of companionship); *Ordinary Mary's Extraordinary Deed* by Emily Pearson (random acts of kindness); *Mr. Peabody's Apples* by Madonna (spreading false rumors); *A Color of His Own*, or *Frederick*, or *Alexander and the Wind-Up Mouse* by Leo Lionni; *The Stamp Collector* by Jennifer Lauthier (censorship, freedom of speech).

Lessons 9–10 (Guided/Independent Practice): How Reading Can Change Your Thinking

This lesson is similar to Lesson 8, but students are now completing the sheet on their own.

- Pass out the Reading Voice/Thinking Voice template on page 148 to students. Begin reading a story aloud, pausing after every few pages. Have students write their summary on the left column and their thinking voice on the right. Allow time for sharing.
- When the story is finished and students have completed both sides of their chart, explain that you want them to try to synthesize their thoughts and ideas about the book:

    Now it is time to show me what matters most to you from this story. What new thoughts do you have? I don't want you to retell the story to me because I just finished reading it—I want to know what you are thinking and what you will remember most about it. What matters to you?

- After they have completed the My Transformed Thoughts box, invite students to share their ideas with each other or with the class.
- Suggested book for this lesson: *Feathers and Fools* by Mem Fox; *I Know a Bear* by Mariana Ruiz Johnson; *The Teddy Bear* by David McPhail; *Stick and Stone* by Beth Ferry; *Whimsy's Heavy Things* by Julia Kraulis; *Faithful Elephants* by Yukio Tsuchiya, *The Dot* or *Ish* by Peter H. Reynolds; *The Three Questions* by Jon Muth; any book by Leo Lionni.

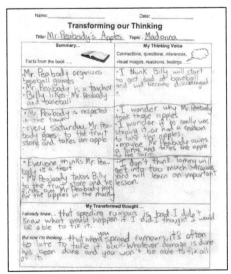

Grade 6 Sample

Lessons 11–12 (Independent Practice): Showing How Books Change Your Thinking

- Have students choose their own books from the Transform book bin and fill out either Reading Voice/Thinking Voice (page 148) or Looking for What Matters Most (page 149) independently.
- Have students share their synthesis of the books with the class.

Lesson 13 (Guided Practice): Looking for Common Themes

This lesson teaches students to pay attention to the big idea or themes from the books.

- Explain that the books were chosen particularly because of the message the author has left.
- Brainstorm some of the themes that students have started to notice from the books.
- Create a class grid of themes and have students record titles under each theme. Some books will, of course, fall under several categories (see themed book lists page 140–142).

Lesson 14: Reflective Journal

Have students record their thoughts about this new strategy and what they've learned about transforming. *How has transforming while you read helped you to understand the story better? Show me or tell me about your thinking.*

Transform for Older Students (Grades 8–12)

For Transform texts to use with older students, see page 142.

After introducing, modeling, and practicing the strategy, use the concept to teach students the literary device of theme. Explain the difference between plot (the events in the story) and theme (a special meaning, message, or thought the author wants reader to take away with them, but is sometimes is not written directly). Provide students with a two-column chart with *Plot* written on the left side, and *Message* written on the right side. Tell them that, while reading, you want them to record the events of the story in the plot column, and any important lessons or learnings in the message column. This is a concrete way of helping students see the difference between plot and meaning.

Assessing Transformed Thinking

NY = Not Yet Meeting Grade Level Expectations
M = Meeting Expectations at a Minimal Level
FM = Fully Meeting Grade Expectations
EX = Exceeding Expectations

Assessing transformed thinking can be challenging, as younger students tend to record either a summary of what happened in the story or a cliché moral they may have heard already. Asking students the key questions *Why do you think the author wrote this book? What did he or she want us to think about?* can really help prompt a response that demonstrates if a student has really understood the deeper meaning of the story.

Transformed Thinking (Synthesize)	NY	M	FM	EX
Understands the difference between a summary (retell) and a synthesis (rethink).				
Can identify the main theme of a story or text.				
Can establish his/her thinking about a topic prior to reading and then revisit the thought afterward, noticing how it might have changed.				
Can identify in writing and/or orally how a book has transformed (changed) his/her thinking.				

Transform Books

Choose titles from the following list of recommended books to use for your modeling and guided lessons and to create a collection for your classroom. You may wish to focus on a particular theme or to select books from a number of different themes.

INJUSTICE, WAR

Bunting, Eve. *Fly Away Home* (P, I)

Bunting, Eve. *Gleam and Glow* (I)

Bunting, Eve. *Smoky Nights* (I)

Bunting, Eve. *The Wall* (I)

Campbell, Nicola. *Shi-Shi-Etko* (I)

Campbell, Nicola. *Shin-Chi's Canoe* (I)

Chikwanine, Michel. *Child Soldier: When Boys and Girls are Used in War* (I)

Cole, Tom Clohosy. *Wall* (I)

Cutler, Jane. *The Cello of Mr. O* (I)

Fox, Mem. *Feathers and Fools* (I)

Gallaz, Christophe. *Rose Blanche* (I)

Garland, Sherry. *The Lotus Seed* (P, I)

Innes, Stephanie. *A Bear in War* (P, I)

Johnston, Tony. *The Harmonica* (I)

Jordan-Fenton, Christy. *Not My Girl* (I)

Jordon-Fenton, Christy. *When I Was Eight* (I)

Lauthier, Jennifer. *The Stamp Collector* (I)

Levine, Ellen. *Henry's Freedom Box* (I)

Pennypacker, Sara. *Sparrow Girl* (I)

Popov, *Why?* (I)

Skarmeta, Antonio. *The Composition* (I)

Tsuchiya, Yukio. *Faithful Elephants: A True Story of Animals, People, and War* (I)

Woodson, Jacqueline. *The Other Side* (I)

FRIENDSHIP, COOPERATION, GETTING ALONG

Chapman, Jared. *Pirate, Viking & Scientist* (P, I)

Dubuc, Marianne. *The Lion and the Bird* (P, I)

Dunklee, Annika. *Me, Too!* (P)

Ferry, Beth. *Stick and Stone* (P, I)

Freedman, Deborah. *By Mouse & Frog* (P)

Freedman, Deborah. *The Story of Fish & Snail* (P)

Henkes, Kevin. *Chester's Way* (P, I)

Janssens, Axel. *The Box* (P, I)

McBratney, Sam. *I'm Sorry* (P)

Oldland, Nicholas. *Walk on the Wild Side* (P, I)

Rosenthal, Amy Krouse. *Friendshape* (P)

Shea, Bob. *Ballet Cat: The Totally Secret Secret* (P)

Willems, Mo. *Can I Play Too?* (P)

Willems, Mo. *City Dog, Country Frog* (P, I)

Willems, Mo. *My Friend is Sad* (P)

Woodson, Jacqueline. *Each Kindness* (I)

CONSERVATION (ENVIRONMENT AND ANIMAL)

Baker, Jeannie. *Window* (P, I)

Brown, Peter. *The Curious Garden* (P, I)

Burningham, John. *Oi! Get Off Our Train* (P, I)

Cherry, Lynne. *The Great Kapok Tree* (I)

Cole, Henry. *On Meadowview Street* (P, I)

DiOrio, Rana. *What Does It Mean to Be Green?* (P, I)

Ering, Timothy Basil. *Frog Belly Rat Bone* (P, I)

Esberger, Trudi. *The Boy Who Lost His Bumble* (P)
Fleming, Denise. *Where Once There Was a Wood* (P)
George, Jean Craighead. *The Last Polar Bear* (P)
James, Simon. *My Friend Whale* (P)
Johnson, Mariana Ruiz. *I Know a Bear* (P)
Kooser, Ted. *House Held Up by Trees* (I)
Seuss, Dr. *The Lorax* (P, I)
Wildsmith, Brian. *Hunter and His Dog* (I)

BULLYING

Alexander, Clair. *Lucy and the Bully* (P)
Bracken, Beth. *The Little Bully* (P)
Cox, Phil Roxbee. *Don't Be A Bully, Billy* (P)
De Kinder, Jan. *Red* (I)
Fraser, Vicki. *Dear Bully of Mine* (P, I)
Ludwig, Trudy. *Just Kidding* (I)
Ludwig, Trudy. *My Secret Bully* (I)
Munson, Derek. *Enemy Pie* (I)
Naylor, Phyllis Reynolds. *King of the Playground* (P, I)
Otoshi, Kathryn. *One* (P, I)
Otoshi, Kathryn. *Two* (P, I)
O'Neill, Alexis. *The Recess Queen* (P)
Polacco, Patricia. *Bully* (I)
Roberts, Justin. *The Smallest Girl in the Smallest Grade* (P, I)
Seeger, Laura Vaccaro. *Bully* (P)
Staake, Bob. *Bluebird* (I)
Woodson, Jacqueline. *Each Kindness* (I)

OVERCOMING CHALLENGES, FACING FEARS

Bromley, Anne C. *The Lunch Thief* (I)
Brown, Marc. *Monkey: Not Ready for Kindergarten* (P)
Brown, Peter. *Mr. Tiger Goes Wild* (P)
Browne, Anthony. *What If?* (P, I)
Button, Lana. *Willow's Whispers* (P)
Castillo, Lauren. *Nana in the City* (P)
Curato, Mike. *Little Elliot, Big City* (P)
Daly, Cathleen. *Emily's Blue Period* (I)
Dismondy, Maria. *Spaghetti in a Hot Dog Bun* (P, I)
Ferrell, Sean. *I Don't Like Koala* (P)
Hale, Bruce. *Clark the Shark* (P)
Henkes, Kevin. *Wemberly Worried* (P, I)
Kraulis, Julia. *Whimsy's Heavy Things* (P, I)
Lionni, Leo. *Swimmy* (P, I)
Liu, Cynthea. *Bike On, Bear!* (P)
Pett, Mark. *The Girl Who Never Made Mistakes* (P, I)
Roberts, Justin. *The Smallest Girl in the Smallest Grade* (P, I)
Schoonmaker, Elizabeth. *Square Cat* (P)
Seeger, Laura Vaccaro. *I Used to Be Afraid* (P)
Snicket, Lemony. *The Dark* (P, I)

Spires, Ashley. *The Most Magnificent Thing* (P, I)
Stead, Philip C. *Lenny & Lucy* (P, I)
Trottier, Maxine. *Migrant* (I)
Uegaki, Chieri. *Hana Hashimoto, Sixth Violin* (P, I)

BELONGING, BEING TRUE TO YOURSELF

Beaty, Andrea. *Rosie Revere, Engineer* (P, I)
DePaola, Tomie. *Oliver Button Is a Sissy* (P, I)
DiPucchio, Kelly. *Gaston* (P, I)
Dyckman, Ame. *Wolfie the Bunny* (P)
Hall, Michael. *Red, A Crayon's Story* (P, I)
Harrison, Hannah. *Extraordinary Jane* (P)
Leaf, Munro. *The Story of Ferdinand* (I)
Lionni, Leo. *Frederick* (P, I)
Lovell, Patty. *Stand Tall, Molly Lou Melon* (P)
Munsch, Robert. *The Paper Bag Princess* (P, I)
O'Leary, Sara. *This is Sadie* (P)
Parr, Todd. *It's Okay to be Different* (P)
Petty, Dev. *I Don't Want to Be A Frog* (P, I)
Reynolds, Peter H. *The Dot* (P, I)
Reynolds, Peter H. *Ish* (P, I)
Shirtliffe, Leanne. *The Change Your Name Store*
Urban, Linda. *Little Red Henry* (P, I)
Watt, Mélanie. *Scaredy Squirrel* (P, I)
Whamond, Dave. *Oddrey* (P, I)
Yolen, Jane. *Not All Princesses Dress in Pink* (P)

GRATITUDE, MINDFULNESS, NOTICING

Carnavas, Peter. *The Boy on the Page* (P)
de la Pena, Matt. *Last Stop on Market Street* (P, I)
DiOrio, Rana. *What Does it Mean to be Present?* (P, I)
Frost, Helen. *Step Gently Out* (P, I)
Frost, Shelley. *I See Kindness Everywhere* (P)
Graham, Bob. *The Silver Button* (P, I)
Graham, Bob. *Vanilla Ice Cream* (P, I)
Lamb, Rosy. *Paul Meets Bernadette* (I)
Lawson, JohnArno. *Sidewalk Flowers* (I)
Maclear, Kyo. *The Specific Ocean* (I)
Magoon, Scott. *Breathe* (P)
Mcleod, Elaine. *Lessons From Mother Earth* (P, I)
Miller, Pat Zietlow. *Wherever You Go* (P)
Portis, Antoinette. *Wait* (P)
Rocco, John. *Blackout* (P, I)
Scanlon, Liz Garton. *All the World* (P, I)
Stinson, Kathy. *The Man With the Violin* (P, I)
Wood, Douglas. *A Quiet Place* (I)

STEWARDSHIP, GIVING BACK, MAKING A DIFFERENCE

Barnett, Mac. *Extra Yarn* (P, I)
Boelts, Maribeth. *Those Shoes* (I)
Brandt, Lois. *Maddi's Fridge* (I)

Cooney, Barbara. *Miss Rumphius* (P, I)
Davies, Nicola. *The Promise* (I)
DiOrio, Rana. *What Does It Mean To Be Kind?* (P, I)
Gavin, Ciara. *Room for Bear* (P)
Gillen, Lynea. *Good People Everywhere* (P, I)
Graham, Bob. *A Bus Called Heaven* (P, I)
Isabella, Jude. *The Red Bicycle: The Extraordinary Story of One Ordinary Bicycle* (I)
Khadra, Mohammed. *Four Feet, Two Sandals* (I)
MacKay, Elly. *Butterfly Park* (P, I)
McPhail, David. *The Teddy Bear* (P, I)
Nelson, Kadir. *If You Plant a Seed* (P)
Pearson, Emily. *Ordinary Mary's Extraordinary Deed* (P, I)
Rath, Tom. *How Full is Your Bucket? For Kids* (P, I)
Stead, Philip C. *A Home For Bird* (P)
Thong, Rosanne. *Fly Free!* (P, I)
Upjohn, Rebecca. *Lily and the Paper Man* (P)

CREATIVITY, IMAGINATION, AMBITION

Belloni, Giulia. *Anything Is Possible* (P)
Clanton, Ben. *Something Extraordinary* (P, I)
Fogliano, Julie. *If You Want to See a Whale* (P, I)
Light, Kelly. *Louise Loves Art* (P)
Meyers, Christopher. *My Pen* (I)
Morris, Richard T. *This Is a Moose* (P)
Morstad, Julie. *How To* (P, I)
O'Leary, Sara. *This is Sadie* (P, I)
Reynolds, Peter H. *Going Places* (P, I)
Reynolds, Peter H. *Sky Color* (P, I)
Spires, Ashley. *The Most Magnificent Thing* (P, I)
Scanlon, Liz Garton. *Think Big* (P)
Yamada, Kobi. *What Do You Do with an Idea?* (P, I)

TECHNOLOGY

Carnavas, Peter. *The Boy on the Page* (I)
Cordell, Matthew. *hello! hello!* (P, I)
Droyd, Ann. *If You Give A Mouse an iPhone: A Cautionary Tale* (P, I)
Droyd, Ann. *Goodnight iPad* (P, I)
Lyon, George Ella. *Book* (P, I)

Mack, Jeff. *Look!* (P)
Miles, David. *Book* (I)
Rocco, John. *Blackout* (I)
Smith, Lane. *It's a Book* (P, I)
Yaccarino, Dan. *Doug Unplugged* (P, I)
Zuckerberg, Randi. *Dot* (I)

BOOKS WITH ABORIGINAL THEMES

Campbell, Nicola. *Shi-Shi-Etko* (I)
Campbell, Nicola. *Shin-Chi's Canoe* (I)
Jordan-Fenton, Christy. *Not My Girl* (I)
Jordon-Fenton, Christy. *When I Was Eight* (I)
Spalding, Andrea. *Secret of the Dance* (I)
Van Camp, Richard. *A Man Called Raven* (I)
Yolen, Jane. *Encounter* (I)

TRANSFORM TEXTS FOR OLDER STUDENTS (GRADES 8–12)

Broun, Heywood. "The Fifty-First Dragon" (short story: courage)
Deal, Borden. "The Taste of Watermelon" (short story: regret)
de Maupassant, Guy. "The Necklace" (short story: greed, truth)
Henry, O. "The Gift of the Magi" (short story: selflessness, kindness)
Jackson, Shirley. "The Lottery" (short story: traditions, customs)
Jackson, Shirley. "The Possibility of Evil" (short story: looks can be deceiving, perception of perfection)
Kotzwinkle, William. "The Curio Shop" (short story: environmental stewardship)
Lawrence, D.H. "The Rocking Horse Winner" (short story: greed)
Madonna. *Mr. Peabody's Apples* (picture book: rumors, truth)
Munsch, Robert. *Love You Forever* (picture book: aging, family)
Robinson, Eden. *Monkey Beach* (novel: *strong content; oppression, colonialism, First Nations)
Vonnegut, Kurt. "Harrison Bergeron" (short story: diversity)

The Language of Transform

Books can **transform** the way we think about

- **Ourselves** (who we are, how we act, what we believe)
- **Others** (and our relationship with them)
- **The world** (and our place in the world)

Key Words for Transform

(use of the *re–* prefix)

- *re-arrange*
- *re-adjust*
- *re-organize*
- *re-visit*
- *re-think*
- *re-construct*

Key Phrases for Transform

- "A transformed thought takes you out of the book and into the world."
- "A thinking adjustment"
- "Ahhhh…. I never thought of it that way before."
- "I always knew that… but now I'm thinking…"
- "A good reader knows that when they are finished reading, they are not finished thinking."
- "A **transformed thought** can change the way you think, act, or feel about yourself, others or the world. "

Noticing Our Thinking Changing

Key Questions to Promote Transformed Thinking

- *What is the moral or message of this story?*
- *Why did the author write this story?*
- *What difference has this book made to me?*
- *How has my thinking changed because of this book?*
- *How has this story changed the way I look at the world?*
- *How has this story changed the way I look at myself?*
- *How has this story made me a better or more understanding person?*

Pembroke Publishers © 2015 *Reading Power, Revised and Expanded* by Adrienne Gear ISBN 978-1-55138-310-1

One Word Activity: Part 1

Name: _____   Date: _____

Take stock of your thinking before you read. Write your one word in the oval; write as many connections as you can around the oval to make a word web.

One Word Activity: Part 2

Name: _____   Date: _____

Revisit your thinking. What are your new thoughts about this word? Write your ideas around the circle to make a web.

Making a Difference

Title: _____

Name _____

In the story, the world is a better place because . . .

I could make the world a better place by . . .

Noticing How My Thinking Changes

Name: _____ Date: _____

Title: _____ Author: _____

My first thought...
_____
_____
_____
_____
_____

On second thought...
_____
_____
_____
_____
_____

My transformed thought...
_____
_____
_____
_____
_____

Pembroke Publishers © 2015 *Reading Power, Revised and Expanded* by Adrienne Gear ISBN 978-1-55138-310-1

Reading Voice/Thinking Voice

Name: _____   Date: _____

Title: _____   Author: _____

My Reading Voice	My Thinking Voice
So far in the story . . . (Summary of what the author wrote)	My connections, questions, inferences, visual images, thoughts, reactions, feelings, etc.
_____	_____
_____	_____
_____	_____
_____	_____
_____	_____

My Transformed Thoughts
What is not written in the story, but now I'm thinking about . . .
(The part that "sticks")

_____

_____

_____

_____

_____

_____

Pembroke Publishers © 2015 *Reading Power, Revised and Expanded* by Adrienne Gear ISBN 978-1-55138-310-1

Looking for What Matters Most

Name: _____ Date: _____

Title: _____ Author: _____

The "big idea" in this book is...

_____

_____

_____

_____

My thoughts, ideas, and opinions about _____ before reading:

_____

_____

_____

_____

But I've changed my mind. Now I think....

_____

_____

_____

_____

What matters most to me is...

_____

_____

_____

_____

Pembroke Publishers © 2015 *Reading Power, Revised and Expanded* by Adrienne Gear ISBN 978-1-55138-310-1

8 Application and Assessment

Although many teachers teach comprehension strategies one at a time, spending several weeks focused on each strategy…this may not be the best way to organize strategy instruction. (Reutzel, Smith, & Fawson, 2005)

And so we come to what is perhaps to the most important chapter in this book: application, or transfer of learning. Our goal with teaching comprehension strategies to students is that they will take what they have learned from our modeling, guiding, and practicing, and they will apply it to their independent reading. But does this actually happen? If it does, how do we know? If it doesn't, what do we do about it? And while I have celebrated over recent years the knowledge that hundreds of teachers are now explicitly teaching comprehension strategies to their students, initially in isolation as I have promoted, the next step is something that requires an equally effective job of promoting.

I wrote: "After students become familiar with all five Reading Power strategies, they are ready to apply their 'busy brains' to any book." My experienced brain now views this statement as rather naive and possibly overly optimistic. I would like to believe that it is that simple, but need to accept the fact that it isn't.

Students Using the Reading Powers

In a recent blog post, the late Grant Wiggins, renowned educator and co-author of the ground-breaking *Understanding By Design*, wrote:

> The lack of transfer of learning of the strategies seems to be a function of inadequate teaching for transfer, and a failure to understand the principles behind the strategies.

If we are to meet our primary goal of supporting our students' independent understanding of texts they read, we need to ensure we are doing everything we can to promote this.

Here are some suggestions for promoting the crucial application or next steps of Reading Power:

- Ensure, by repeatedly checking over time, that students know what the goal is: to successfully apply any or all Reading Power strategies every time they read any text.
- Continually promote the transfer of learning of comprehension strategies to all classroom tasks in a variety of different contexts (different subject areas) and different texts (fiction, nonfiction, read-alouds, newspaper articles, etc.) so that students learn that the strategies of thinking can be applied to all reading experiences; e.g., they are not to just make connections with a Connect book.
- Create an anchor chart with comprehension prompts and post it in the classroom.

Song lyrics are an engaging way for students to apply their reading power strategies. Grade 6 students at my school chose a current song (with appropriate lyrics) and created PowerPoint presentations with slides showing their connections, questions, visual images, inferences, and transformed thinking.

Pay attention to your thinking voice...

Your thinking voice says	Reading Power
This reminds me of...	Connect
I'm wondering... (why? how? when? what? who?)	Question
I can see this in my mind...	Visualize
Maybe... (this is what I think is going to happen next)	Predict
Maybe... (this isn't in the book, but now I'm thinking...)	Infer
So far...	Summary
This is important...	Main Idea
Now I'm thinking...	Transform

Allowing students to choose already familiar charts and templates (BlackLine Masters or BLMs) to extend their thinking on paper is another way to encourage application of these strategies, and provides students with different ways to show their thinking.

- Provide regular opportunities for students to choose their own books and encourage them to practice a repertoire of strategies during independent reading. (Sticky notes for recording thinking should be available but optional.)
- Model the difference between metacognition (being aware of thinking as you read) and self-monitoring (knowing when you are not getting it).
- Choose challenging texts for guided practice to nudge thinking forward.
- Teach two strategies back-to-back to demonstrate how strategies work together; i.e., connecting with visualizing or questioning with inferring.
- Discuss how readers can choose the strategy that supports their thinking for the particular text they are reading. Model this regularly.
- Provide opportunities for formative assessment, gradually decreasing the number of prompts. Encourage students to self-analyze use of strategies.
- Gradually stop isolating the strategies by modeling how a good reader is able to use all five strategies intermittently while they read.
- Use the What? So What? template on page 152 or Using My Reading Powers on page 153 to have students practice using these strategies while they read. Older and more competent readers could begin to code their thinking voice by marking their thoughts with the letters of the strategies used.

Most Transform books can be used to practice the different strategies or Powers.

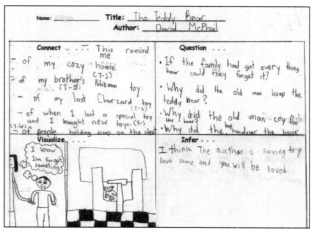

Grade 4 Sample

What? So What?

Name: _____

Date: _____

Title: _____

Author: _____

What? What happened so far in the story? (Summary of what the author wrote)	**So What?** What do I think about the story? (connections, questions, thoughts, inferences.)

Pembroke Publishers © 2015 *Reading Power, Revised and Expanded* by Adrienne Gear ISBN 978-1-55138-310-1

Using My Reading Powers

Name: _____   Date: _____

Title:_____   Author: _____

My connections	My questions
_____	_____
_____	_____
_____	_____
_____	_____
_____	_____
_____	_____
What I visualized	**My inferences**
_____	_____
_____	_____
_____	_____
_____	_____
_____	_____
_____	_____

My transformed thought

_____

_____

_____

Pembroke Publishers © 2015 *Reading Power, Revised and Expanded* by Adrienne Gear ISBN 978-1-55138-310-1

Reading Power and Literature Circles

Literature circles or novel studies are excellent opportunities for older students to utilize and apply their reading powers with more complex texts. It also allows us to observe how well our students are able to transfer their understanding of individual strategies to a drawing from a repertoire of strategies when reading independently.

Literature circles provides opportunities for students to

- have a more meaningful, interactive, and enjoyable reading experience.
- draw from their repertoire of known reading strategies and apply them independently.
- gain a deeper understanding of the book than if they had answered comprehension questions after every chapter.
- read and work independently.
- engage in authentic, small-group discussions about their novels.
- read rich, thought-provoking novels.

I have started choosing books for literature circles that focus on a common theme but are at a variety of reading levels. This allows us to have whole-class discussions about the theme but also makes sure students are reading books at their reading level. See the book list pages 169–170 for suggested themes.

While my past experience with literature circles had not proven very successful, Reading Power has allowed me to fine tune the structure and organization so that students became more engaged in the reading, thinking, and discussing of the books in a more authentic way. Students who have been exposed to the language of thinking by learning and practicing the Reading Power strategies with picture books can begin to use these strategies with more sophisticated texts. Their literature circles look, sound, and feel more like legitimate book-club discussions, rather than the forced talk that tends to come from the assigned roles traditional to literature circles. I recommend doing a whole-class novel first, which allows you to model and explain your expectations and provides opportunities for more guidance and monitoring. Once students are familiar with the structure of the novel study, they will be able to work through their Literature Circle discussions and activities with more confidence.

Recommended Year Plan

Term 1
- Reading Power strategies are taught (or reviewed) using picture books

Term 2
- Whole-class novel: teacher guides students through format
- Students meet in small groups weekly, but all are discussing the same book
- Teacher provides mini-lessons for additional response activities

Term 3
- Lit circles: students are grouped according to reading level; each group has a different book (sometimes with a similar theme; e.g., children in war/ overcoming adversity/children in slavery).
- Students work more independently because they are more familiar with the format and activities.

Weekly Thinking Page, Grade 4 Sample

Each week, I assign a certain number of pages or chapters, and students are responsible for reading and using sticky notes to mark up to three passages where they noticed their thinking voice while reading: i.e., a connection, question, visual image, inference, or new thought. I meet with each group once a week to discuss the previous chapter(s). Students come to lit circle discussions prepared to share; they take turns sharing their passages and their thinking in the group. More proficient readers might also be able to identify which strategies they used. Other students in the group can then contribute their own comments or thoughts to the discussion. If two students have chosen the same passage, a comparison of their thinking can be part of the discussion.

Here are some examples from a group of Grade 4 students who were discussing the novel *Stone Fox* by John Reynolds Gardiner:

- "When I read this part, it reminded me of the time that my grandpa was very sick and he had to go to the hospital. He couldn't get out of bed and it made me feel so scared and sad all mixed together." (Connect)
- "When I read this part, it made really clear pictures in my mind. The words that really helped me create my pictures were…. I drew a picture of it." (Visualize)
- "When I read this part I was thinking that maybe Willy would change his mind about entering the dog sled race after he saw Stone Fox's team. That was an inference, I think, because my brain said '"maybe'." (Inference)
- "When I read this part, I was really confused. I mean, how could Willy actually think that he would win when he only had one dog and everyone else had a whole team of dogs?" (Question)

Before You Start

- Group your class into three to five ability groups, based on reading assessments.
- If possible, arrange for a support teacher, librarian, or parent volunteer to be involved and take one of the groups.
- Block off two one-hour blocks in your weekly schedule.
- Select an appropriate leveled novel for each group—and read them!
- Divide each novel into 6–8 (depending on how long you wish to spend) equal sections (note page numbers) to ensure that everyone finishes their book at the same time. Some books divide by chapters, others by pages.

Sample of Lit Circle Set-Up

Novel: *The Lemonade War*

Week 1	Week 2	Week 3	Week 4	Week 5	Week 6	Week 7	Week 8
Pages/chapter 3–15	Pages/chapter 16–28	Pages/chapter 29–36	Pages/chapter	Pages/chapter	Pages/chapter	Pages/chapter	Pages/chapter

Getting Started

- Choose one word connected to each novel.
- Do the One Word activity (see page 134 for lesson and template on page 144) with your class.
- Give each student a lit circle booklet and a small stack of sticky notes.
- Review weekly assignments (I like to make an anchor chart).
  - Read assigned pages.
  - While reading, stick 1–3 sticky notes into the book and record your thinking.
  - Come to weekly lit circle discussion prepared to share one of your passages and your thinking.
  - Complete one Weekly Thinking Page (see page 159 for template).
  - Additional Response Activity: do one per week (see below).
- Assessment will be based on
  1. Weekly written work and lit circle booklets (teacher marks).
  2. Preparation for weekly lit circle meetings: reading, marking thinking passages, and discussion during lit circle (teacher keeps track of student progress on Lit Circle Discussion Record, page 158).

Additional Response Activities

CHARACTERS I WILL MEET

As new characters are introduced, students record their names, who they are, a picture, and personality traits describing them(see organizer on page 160).

CHARACTER VENN

Students compare themselves with the main character. Words should include both descriptors of themselves—e.g., *girl*, *only child*, *plays hockey*—and personality traits—e.g., *brave*, *funny*, *kind* (see template on page 161).

SETTING MAP

Students draw, label, and color a map of the setting of the book, showing a bird's-eye view and including the places mentioned in the book (see template on page 162).

PHOTO ALBUM

Students illustrate the book. They choose five moments/events/images to draw and color, including a caption and page number (see organizer on page 163).

I always give class time for students to read, prepare their sticky notes, and work on their additional activities. During this time, I meet with each group individually for our weekly discussions. Use the Lit Circle Discussion record (page 158) to track student progress during these discussions.

As part of the established assignment, each student does one new activity per week.

Grade 6 Sample

TRANSFORMING MY THINKING

Students complete the organizer on page 164. They will need to have had some previous background and practice with the Transform strategy. Remind them to include how their thinking has changed now that they have finished reading.

LETTER TO THE AUTHOR

Students write a letter to the author. The letter should include an introductory paragraph introducing themselves to the author, their response/reaction to the book, the parts they liked and why, and their personal connections. Students can use the instructions on page 165 and the template on page 166.

VOCABULARY PAGE

Students record any new words they encounter during reading. Definitions and sentences for each word should be included on the New Words page (page 167).

TITLE PAGE

Students create a front cover for their package, including the title of the novel (encourage block or 3D lettering), the student's name, a border, and colored illustrations. Remind them not to copy the pictures from the cover of the book.

Lit Circle Assessment

When assessing lit circles, I like to evaluate both the students' written work and their effort during discussions. To use the Lit Circle Discussion Record (page 158), copy one table per student. Use the table to track individual student progress during weekly meetings. Rotate through the groups and listen as students share their passages and thinking. I find this record a helpful reference when I'm doing my term assessments. When the students have finished reading their novels and completed all the lit circle activities, I use the Rubric on page 158 to provide them with feedback. This rubric was designed to reflect students' performance in both written work and participation in the weekly discussions.

Recommended Books for Lit Circles

The bottom line is that the success of literature circles is fully dependent on the novels you choose for your students to read. Great discussions about books are born from great books. There is no shortage of great books out there—books that make you sigh or cry or shout and shake your head and shake your fist or hug your friend; books to savor and to keep under your pillow because, even when you are finished reading it, you want to keep it near you. Let your children experience these feelings with the books they are reading. They will love you for it. So ask your Parent Advisory Council or apply for a grant and spend a few dollars on some new novel sets. I cannot think of a better way to spend your money.

On pages 168–170 are my recommendations for novels to use for novel studies and/or literature circles. I have grouped them by grade level and listed themes for each book, but only you can tell if they are in line with your students' reading levels. It is important that you preread these books to ensure that the level, content, and language are appropriate for your students. Please note that some are recently published and might be available only in hard cover at the time of publishing; to deal with the extra expense, these could be used as a read-aloud novel study.

Lit Circle Discussion Record

Student:	Date:										TOTAL:
_____	**Passage /5 Selection:**										
Novel:	**Individual /5 Sharing:**										
_____	**Group /5 Participation:**										
Comments:											

Lit Circle Assessment Rubric

NAME:	NM	M	FM	EX
Comes to Lit Circle prepared with a thoughtful passage to share and readily contributes to the group discussions.				
Applies a variety of comprehension strategies while reading his/her novel, such as making connections, visualizing, and questioning.				
Demonstrates both a literal (retell) and inferential (rethink) understanding of their novel.				

Weekly Thinking Page

Name: _____   Date: _____

Chapter: _____   Pages: _____

So far… (tell briefly what happened in this chapter)	This reminds me of… (tell about any connections you have to the story or character)
_____ _____ _____ _____ _____	_____ _____ _____ _____
I'm wondering… (write 3–4 deep-thinking questions you have about this chapter)	Maybe… (answer one or two of your questions by inferring or predicting)
_____ _____ _____ _____	_____ _____ _____ _____
My strongest image: (sketch one image and label or write a sentence telling about it)	I think… (make a prediction of what you think might happen in the next chapter. Explain why you think this.)
	_____ _____ _____ _____

Pembroke Publishers © 2015 *Reading Power, Revised and Expanded* by Adrienne Gear ISBN 978-1-55138-310-1

Characters I Will Meet

Name: _____   Date: _____

Name of character: _____ **Who is he/she?** _____ **Personality traits: (describe what this character is like)** _____ _____ _____	**Draw and color a picture of this character:**
Name of character: _____ **Who is he/she?** _____ **Personality traits: (describe what this character is like)** _____ _____ _____	**Draw and color a picture of this character**

Pembroke Publishers © 2015 *Reading Power, Revised and Expanded* by Adrienne Gear ISBN 978-1-55138-310-1

Character Venn

Name: _____

Date: _____

Create a Venn diagram, comparing **yourself** with the **main character** of your book. Include basic information such as gender, family, school, age, interests, and talents, as well as personality traits.

Main Character

Me

Setting Map

Name: _____   Date: _____

In the space below, design a map showing the setting of your story. Include the important places that are included in the book. **Color** and **label** your map.

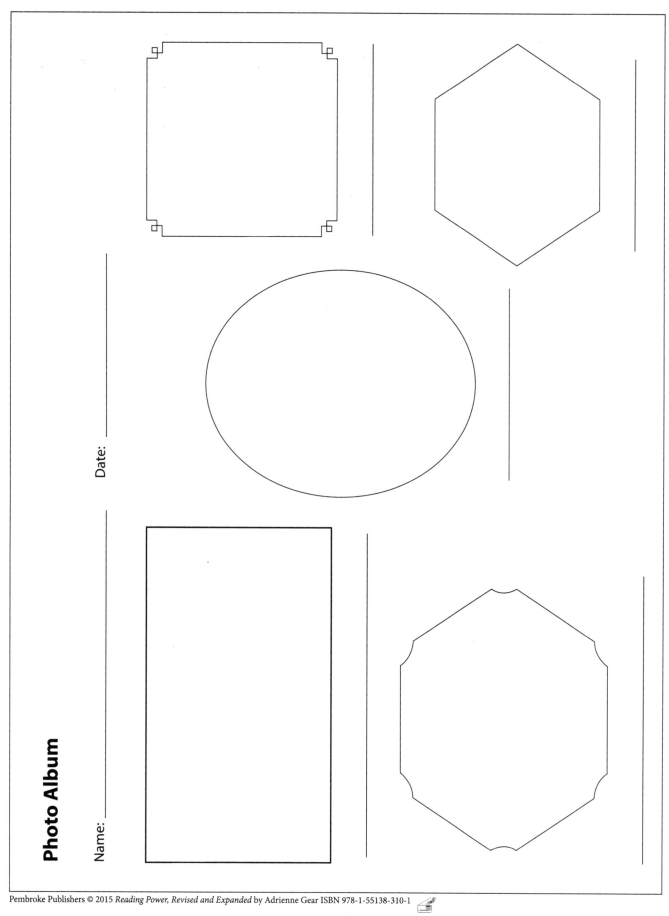

Photo Album

Name: _____

Date: _____

Pembroke Publishers © 2015 *Reading Power, Revised and Expanded* by Adrienne Gear ISBN 978-1-55138-310-1

Transforming My Thinking

Name: _____   Date: _____

Title: _____   Author: _____

At first I thought this book was about…

_____

_____

_____

_____

But then I realized that it was about…

_____

_____

_____

_____

I think the author wrote this book because he/she wanted us to think about…

_____

_____

_____

_____

I already knew that…

_____

_____

But this book has changed the way I think about…

_____

_____

Pembroke Publishers © 2015 *Reading Power, Revised and Expanded* by Adrienne Gear ISBN 978-1-55138-310-1

Letter to the Author

Name: _____ Date: _____

Once you have finished reading your novel, write a letter to author about their book. Your letter should include

- the date

- a greeting

- a brief introduction to yourself (name, age, school)

- the title of the book you read and how you came to read it (e.g., read it in class in a lit circle)

- your opinion of the book

- your favorite part and why

- your favorite character and why

- connections you made to the story

- something that surprised you

- questions you would like to ask the author

- a closing (thank author for writing, etc.)

- your signature

Letter to the Author, cont'd

_____

Dear _____ ,

_____

_____

_____

_____

_____

_____

_____

_____

_____

_____

_____

_____

_____

_____

_____

_____

New Words

Name: _____ Date: _____

Title: _____ Author: _____

New word: _____ page: _____

Definition: _____

Sentence: _____

New word: _____ page: _____

Definition: _____

Sentence: _____

New word: _____ page: _____

Definition: _____

Sentence: _____

New word: _____ page: _____

Definition: _____

Sentence: _____

Pembroke Publishers © 2015 *Reading Power, Revised and Expanded* by Adrienne Gear ISBN 978-1-55138-310-1

GRADES 2–3

Bates, Sonya Spreen. *Wildcat Run* (ski trip, lost, survival)

Davis, Tony. *Roland Wright: Future Knight* (knight in training)

DeCamillo, Kate. *Leroy Ninker Saddles Up* (wanna-be cowboy and his horse)

Estes, Eleanor. *The Hundred Dresses* (bullying, friendship, forgiveness)

Gannett, Ruth Stiles. *My Father's Dragon* (fantasy, boy tries to rescue dragon)

Hale, Shannon. *Princess in Black* (princess turned superhero, humor)

Hanlon, Abby. *Dory Fantasmagory* (family, youngest sibling, humor, imagination)

Himmelman, John. *Tales of Bunjitsu* Bunny (short stories, martial arts, Eastern philosophy)

Jenkins, Emily. *Toys Go Out* (*Toy Story* characters, adventure)

Lagercrantz, Rose. *My Happy Life* (school, friendship, best friend moves away)

Viorst, Judith. *Lulu and the Brontosaurus* (humor, adventure, girl searches for pet brontosaurus)

GRADES 3–4

Dahl, Roald. *Fantastic Mr. Fox* (clever fox outwitting farmers)

Davies, Jacqueline. *The Lemonade War* (siblings, lemonade-stand challenge)

Gardiner, John Reynolds. *Stone Fox* (boy tries to win dogsled race to save family farm)

Henkes, Kevin. *The Year of Billy Miller* (realistic, funny; school, family, friends)

Jonell, Lynne. *Emmy and the Incredible Shrinking Rat* (mystery, magic, real-life problems, humor)

MacLachlan, Patricia. *Waiting for the Magic* (father leaves, family, pets, magic, love)

Messner, Kate. *Marty McGuire* (tomboy character, friendship, school)

GRADE 4

Birney, Betty G. *The World According to Humphrey* (class pet guinea pig tells the story)

Blume, Judy. *Tales of a Fourth Grade Nothing* (hilarious mishaps of boy and his younger brother)

Catling, Patrick Skene. *The Chocolate Touch* (boy is cursed)

DiCamillo, Kate. *The Miraculous Journey of Edward Tulane* (rabbit adventure, hope, love)

Graff, Graff. *Double Dog Dare* (mean girls)

Houston, James. *Tikta'Liktak: An Inuit Legend* (young Inuit, survival story)

Jennings, Patrick. *Guinea Dog* (family guinea pig thinks he's a dog)

Jonell, Lynne. *The Sign of the Cat* (fantasy on the high seas, talking cats, adventure)

Jones, Kelly. *Unusual Chickens for the Exceptional Poultry Farmer* (humor, girl moves to farm, cares for supernatural chickens)

Levy, Dana Alison. *The Misadventures of the Family Fletcher* (family, taking risks, making choices)

Lin, Grace. *The Year of the Dog* (family, school, immigration)

GRADE 5

Applegate, Katherine. *The One and Only Ivan* (shopping mall, gorilla tells his story)

Baird, Alison. *The Dragon's Egg* (magic, girl has pet dragon, bullying)

Creech, Sharon. *The Boy on the Porch* (couple finds a gifted boy)

Grabenstein, Chris. *Escape from Mr. Lemoncello's Library* (*Night at the Museum/Chocolate Factory*)

Graff, Lisa. *Absolutely Almost* (bully/bullied/bystander, friendship, family)

Hunt, Lynda Mullaly. *One for the Murphys* (foster child finding love)

Lloyd, Natalie. *A Snicker of Magic* (magical realism)

Messner, Kate. *All the Answers* (magical realism, anxiety, magic pencil)

Oppel, Kenneth. *The Boundless* (adventure on train, Canadian history and historical figures)

Sacher, Louis. *Holes* (boy in juvenile camp digging a hole, great characters)

Salerni, Dianne K. *The Eighth Day* (adventure, fantasy, discovery of extra day of the week, King Arthur)

GRADE 6

Anderson, Jeff. *Zack Delacruz: Me and My Big Mouth* (school, friendship, bully, teamwork)

Bacigalupi, Paola. *Zombie Baseball Beatdown* (food safety, racism, baseball)

Beasley, Cassie. *Circus Mirandus* (magic, fantasy, circus)

Bertman, Jennifer Chambliss. *Book Scavenger* (puzzles, mystery, travel, books)

Forester, Victoria. *The Girl Who Could Fly* (adventure, fantasy, magic realism, courage)

Graff, Lisa. *Lost in the Sun* (boy struggles to move on after tragic accident)

Holm, Jennifer L. *The Fourteenth Goldfish* (11-year-old, change, family relationships, science)

Martin, Ann M. *Rain Reign* (Asperger's syndrome, OCD, obsession with homonyms, dog)

Messner, Kate. *Wake Up Missing* (suspense, tweens, concussion, identity theft)

Nielsen, Jennifer. *The False Prince* (medieval adventure)

Palacio, R.J. *Wonder* (disfigured boy adjusting to school, bullying, courage)

Paulsen, Gary. *The Hatchet* (survival, adventure, boy survives alone after plane crash)

Scanlon, Liz Garton. *The Great Good Summer* (girl abandoned by mother, friendship, faith, adventure)

Shurtliff, Liesl. *Rump: The True Story of Rumpelstiltskin* (fantasy, humor)

Spinelli, Jerry. *Maniac Magee* (realistic/legend, survival, racism)

GRADES 6–7

Arnold, Elana K. *The Question of Miracles* (moving story of loss, death, fears and miracles)

Bell, Cece. *El Deafo* (graphic novel/memoir of young girl with hearing impairment)

Bruchac, Joseph. *The Warriors* (aboriginal boy, family, culture, school, lacrosse)

Buyea, Rob. *Because of Mr. Terrupt* (teacher, students, accident)

Cotter, Charis. *The Swallow: A Ghost Story* (1960s Toronto, mystery, family)

Ellis, Deborah. *The Breadwinner* (challenges facing young girl in war-torn Afghanistan)

Foxlee, Karen. *Ophelia and the Marvelous Boy* (story within a story, modern-day character weaves into fairy tale)

Gemeinhart, Dan. *The Honest Truth* (poignant, uplifting, boy battling terminal illness, friendship, family)

Graff, Lisa. *A Tangle of Knots* (mystery, magical talent, baking, multiple voices)

Hopkinson, Deborah. *The Great Trouble: A Mystery of London, The Blue Death, and a Boy Called Eel* (historical fiction, cholera, mystery)

Hunt, Lynda Mullaly. *Fish in a Tree* (girl with dyslexia, inspiring teacher, friendship)

Lamana, Julie T. *Upside Down in the Middle of Nowhere* (realistic, Hurricane Katrina, disaster)

Lord, Cynthia. *Rules* (girl makes rules for her autistic brother)

Turner, Amber McRee. *Circa Now* (girl, old photographs, mystery)

GRADE 7 AND UP

Alexander, Kwame. *The Crossover* (twins, basketball, written in verse)

Draper, Sharon. *Out of My Mind* (cerebral palsy)

Falcone, L.M. *Walking with the Dead* (adventure, ancient Greece)

Holczer, Tracy. *The Secret Hum of a Daisy* (girl, home, loss, grief, clues)

Jamieson, Victoria. *Roller Girl* (graphic novel, coming of age, finding your passion, roller derby)

Jordan-Fenton, Christy. *Fatty Legs: A True Story* (residential school)

Loftin, Nikki. *Nightingale's Nest* (boy befriends magical singing girl, forced to make decision, Hans Christian Andersen)

Lowry, Lois. *The Giver* (dystopia, memory keeper)

Mikaelsen, Ben. *Touching Spirit Bear* (aboriginal, delinquent sent to island, survival)

Nelson, Jandy *I'll Give You the Sun* (twins, two voices, love, grief, family)

Ryan, Pam Munoz. *Echo* (music, magic, courage, family, fantasy, historical fiction)

Taylor, Theodore. *The Cay* (white boy and black man stranded on island, survival, racism)

Woodson, Jacqueline. *Brown Girl Dreaming* (African-American, 1960–70s civil rights movement, told in verse)

Lir Circle Books by Theme for Middle-Grade

CHILDREN OVERCOMING ADVERSITY

Bell, Cece. *El Deafo* (hearing impairment)

Draper, Sharon. *Out of My Mind* (cerebral palsy)

Graff, Lisa. *Absolutely Almost* (struggling reader)

Lord, Cynthia. *Rules* (autistic brother)

Martin, Ann M. *Rain Reign* (Asperger's syndrome, OCD)

Palacio, R.J. *Wonder* (physical deformity)

Sloan, Holly Goldberg. *Counting By 7s* (genius, social issues)

Vawter, Vince. *Paperboy* (stutter)

CHILDREN IN THIRD-WORLD COUNTRIES

D'Adamo, Francesco. *Iqbal*

Ellis, Deborah. *I Am a Taxi*

Grindley, Sally. *Bitter Chocolate*

Laird, Elizabeth. *The Garbage King*

Park, Linda Sue. *A Long Walk to Water*

Pinkney, Andrea Davis. *The Red Pencil*

RESIDENTIAL SCHOOLS

Jordan-Fenton, Christy. *Fatty Legs: A True Story*

Jordan-Fenton, Christy. *A Stranger at Home: A True Story*

Loyie, Larry. *As Long as the Rivers Flow*

Loyie, Larry. *Goodbye Buffalo Bay*

Robertson, David Alexander. *Sugar Falls* (graphic novel)

Robertson, David Alexander. *Ends/Begins* (graphic novel)

Sterling, Shirley. *My Name is Seepeetza*

CHILDREN IN WAR

Boyne, John. *The Boy in the Striped Pajamas* (Holocaust)

Bradley, Kimberly Brubaker. *The War That Saved My Life* (WWII)

Dauvillier, Loic. *Hidden: A Child's Story of the Holocaust* (graphic novel)

Dowsell, Paul. *Sektion 20* (Holocaust)

Ellis, Deborah. *The Breadwinner* (Afghanistan)

Laird, Elizabeth. *Oranges in No Man's Land* (Beirut)

Lowry, Lois. *Number the Stars* (Holocaust)

Mankell, Henning. *Secrets in the Fire* (Mozambique)

McSwigan, Marie. *Snow Treasure* (WWII)

Meyer, Susan Lynn. *Black Radishes* (Holocaust)

Senzai, N.H. *Shooting Kabul* (Afghanistan)

Yelchin, Eugene. *Breaking Stalin's Nose* (Soviet dictatorship)

Reading Power and Parents

"Children are made readers on the laps of their parents."
—Emilie Buchwald, author

"Kids not only need to read a lot but they need lots of books they can read right at their fingertips. They also need access to books that entice them, attract them to reading. Schools… can make it easy and unrisky for children to take books for the evening or weekend by worrying less about losing books to children and more about losing children to literacy."
—Richard Allington, *What Really Matters for Struggling Readers*

Reading at home with your child has long been regarded as one of the most important things parents can do to assist in their child's learning. In my experience, most parents, when reading at home with their beginning reader, do what many of us in the teaching profession have been guilty of: they concentrate on the code, on the saying of the words, and often forget about the comprehension. Learning to read, in the eyes of many parents, is learning to say the words on the page. Introducing parents to Reading Power—the concepts of strategic thinking, making meaning, metacognition, and the language of thinking—will help guide their support away from a focus on decoding towards a more balanced understanding of what being a reader is.

I believe parents have the best intentions when reading at home with their children, but they might not know how to move beyond helping their child say the words on the page. Parents I have worked with over the years are eager to know how they can help their children learn to read—they just need to be shown how. Providing a simple strategy with simple language that they can use at home gives them practical tools to help their child read.

During the years that I have taught Reading Power, I have been invited to many parent nights, PAC meetings, and Family Literacy celebrations. I show up with my Reading Power poster and a tub of books, and proceed to give parents a brief overview of the research and the concept of metacognition, explaining each strategy. I then model, with a picture book, what reading at home with their child might look like and sound like, modeling a read-aloud/think-aloud with Reading Power strategies and language. The response has been extremely positive; parents are grateful to have this new understanding and are eager to try it at home with their child. Many parents have told me how much more enjoyable the experience is now that they know what to do, and have commented on how much their children enjoy hearing their connections.

If you school is planning to implement Reading Power strategies, it is important that members of your parent community understand what Reading Power is and how they can practice some of the strategies at home. Websites, newsletters, notices home, and parent information nights are some of the ways that your parents can become informed.

Some schools create bookmarks to pass out during parent night as a take-home reminder of strategies. The bookmarks can include some key points of Reading Power and a list of some of the thinking prompts (see page 174); the information on the Home Reading Sheets (pages 175–179) can also be used for bookmarks.

Parent Night

Host a parent evening and invite one or two staff members to present a brief overview of Reading Power. Include a model lesson on how to do a read-aloud/think-aloud, so parents can use the strategies when reading at home with their child. The Reading Power parent information sheet (page 174) or copies of the Home Reading Sheets (pages 175–179) could be distributed during this presentation. Have a collection of recommended Reading Power books for parents to view.

Morning Reading

If parents are involved in morning reading in your classroom, encourage parent and child to practice Reading Power strategies together. You can post the specific strategy the class is working on and children can teach their parents how to use the strategy with the book they are reading together.

School Newsletters

Include information about Reading Power in monthly newsletters. The Reading Power parent information sheet (page 174) could be included in a fall school newsletter or in the first-term report-card overview. Include book recommendations and student samples in the newsletter.

Strategy of the Month

Promote a Strategy of the Month in the school newsletter. Include book recommendations and an overview of the strategy. Your principal can announce the focus strategy at the beginning of the month, and even incorporate the language of thinking into daily announcements: "I'm inferring from the view from my office window that it will be an inside recess today." Students can share Reading Power books or lessons at the monthly assembly and invite parents to watch.

Home Reading

I know that regular reading at home is an essential part of a child's successful development as a reader, but I have always struggled with home reading programs that include laborious reading logs, parent signatures, and daily checks. Using Reading Power to promote an interactive home reading program—child and parent interacting with each other; child and parent interacting with the book—is a much more effective and realistic approach. The key to making this successful for parent, child, and teacher is to be realistic about your expectations. Once a week, invite students to choose a book (from the book box, library, class collection) to take home and read with their parents. Together, they practice one or more Reading Power strategies. After parent and child interact with the story by reading and thinking together, they work together to complete the appropriate Home Reading Sheet (pages 175–179).

Reading Power Book of the Month

As part of the Home Reading program, you might choose one special book to be passed from student to student during the course of one month. The same book is circulated throughout the class, each student taking a turn at bringing it home, reading it with parents, and completing a Home Reading Sheet with parents. The book is then brought back to school and passed on to a classmate. At the end of the month, the Home Reading Sheets can be displayed outside the classroom, along with the jacket of the book. Parents and students will enjoy reading everyone's different connections to the same book.

Assessment

Assessment needs to be reflective of our goals and help to inform our practice. If our goal as teachers is that our students are able to read a passage and correctly answer a series of comprehension questions, then our assessment needs to reflect that. Many traditional assessments of reading comprehension do just that: provide students with passages to read and questions to be answered. And while valuable information about our students' comprehension can be gained from these formal assessment tools, I believe it is also important for teachers to look beyond whether or not a student is getting the right answer, to try to evaluate *how* they are getting those answers. There is a need, therefore, to reassess our reading goals for our students in order to better assess their comprehension skills and help guide our practice.

It is essential not to confuse our assessment of thinking with our assessment of other skills. Struggling decoders are not necessarily struggling thinkers; written output is rarely a reflection of cognitive ability. Students who struggle with written output or decoding of text should still be given a chance to demonstrate their thinking. We need to find alternative ways to assess these students, to ensure we are assessing their thinking and not their writing or decoding. This might mean making adjustments to how we assess certain students: e.g., reading aloud for those who struggle with code, or scribing for students who struggle with written output.

Goals of Reading Comprehension

As a teacher of reading, my goals for my students are that they

- develop an awareness of thinking; become metacognitive.
- develop a language of thinking to articulate their understanding of the text.
- identify and apply a variety thinking strategies to the texts they are reading independently.
- understand and be able to explain how and why specific strategies can be used to deepen their understanding of the text.

ASSESSING THE GOALS

The Reading Power Questionnaire (page 180) will help assess the first goal—have students developed an awareness of their thinking, or become metacognitive learners? I like to give this questionnaire early in September to assess where my students are in their understanding of metacognition. If it is your first year teaching Reading Power, you will likely find that many of your students are not familiar with the strategies; if your school has already implemented this common language of comprehension, the students you receive in the fall will already have been exposed to some of the strategies. The questionnaire will provide you with insight to guide your teaching, and will help you establish which strategies you need to focus on and for how long. For example, if most of your class already knows and is able to make connections, then you likely do not need to be spending as much time on the Connect strategy. Towards the end of the school year, I give the class the same questionnaire and then compare each individual's results to see where growth has taken place.

INFORMAL ASSESSMENT

Informal evaluation provides us with invaluable insight into our student progress. The Reading Power Checklist on page 181, created by a teacher in Richmond, is an informal list you can keep close by during direct and guided lessons. When you begin to recognize students who are demonstrating an understanding of a particular strategy, you can jot down quick comments or check beside their names. Similarly, if you see that a student is struggling to understand a strategy, a quick note beside the student's name will remind you that this child might need extra support.

FORMAL ASSESSMENT

When you want to go deeper into an individual student's understanding of each of the Reading Powers, the Comprehension Assessment on page 182 can be used. This can be used as an interview with each student after a strategy is taught, or as a whole-class assessment. In the case of a whole class-assessment, you might want to choose one story to read aloud and then have students write their responses. For primary students, you might need to read the questions aloud and leave time in between for them to write their responses.

This form can be used for ongoing assessment: students fill out only the portion of the sheet pertaining to the most recently taught strategy. Or, for students familiar with all the strategies, it can be given periodically throughout the year. Noticing the gaps in the students' understanding of certain strategies will help to guide your practice and show you which Reading Powers require more teaching.

The rubric is written using child-friendly descriptors and so can be used for both student self-assessment and teacher assessment.

The Reading Power Rubric on pages 183 and 184 outlines, in child-friendly language on a four-point scale, the levels of demonstration, understanding, and output for each of the five Reading Powers. These are not provincial performance standards, but were created as common standards for assessing and reporting these five comprehension strategies. They can be used by the teacher for student assessment or by the student for self-assessment.

Reading Power

Helping Your Children Become
More Powerful Readers and Thinkers

A Guide for Parents

"Meaning is constructed in the realm where readers meet the words in the text and consider the ideas in terms of their own experience and knowledge."

—Stephanie Harvey

What is Reading Power?

Reading Power is a research-based approach to comprehension instruction that we are implementing at _____school. In order for children to develop as proficient readers, they must learn and practice both the strategies of decoding (learning to read the words) and the strategies of thinking (learning to make sense of the words). *Reading Power* is a way of helping students develop important comprehension skills to become more powerful readers and thinkers.

The five comprehension strategies, or reading powers, we are teaching are:

1. **Connect:** What does the story remind me of?

2. **Visualize:** What pictures can I make in my head from this story?

3. **Question:** What am I wondering about this story?

4. **Infer:** What am I thinking about this story that isn't actually written?

5. **Transform:** How has my thinking changed because of this story?

What are the Key Ideas?
- Learning to read involves two distinct, yet equally important components:
    Decoding: the ability to read the words on the page with fluency and accuracy
    Comprehension: the ability to construct meaning from the text
- Comprehension strategies need to be **taught directly** and explicitly so that students can understand what thinking looks like and sounds like.
- **Common language** of these thinking strategies is essential for helping students acquire the "language of thinking" across the grades.
- **Metacognition**, or "awareness of thinking," is an important component of this program
- We have two voices: a **speaking voice** and a **thinking voice**. Good readers pay attention to their **thinking voice** while they read.
- Teachers and parents can **model** their **thinking voice** while they read to and with their children, to help teach and reinforce the strategies

---

Pembroke Publishers © 2015 *Reading Power, Revised and Expanded* by Adrienne Gear ISBN 978-1-55138-310-1

Reading Power Home Reading Sheet: Connect

"Good reader make CONNECTIONS while they read!"

Name: _____   Date: _____

Title: _____

Author: _____

My connection:

This book reminds me of....

_____

_____

_____

_____

My _____'s connection   :

This book reminds me of....

_____

_____

_____

_____

Pembroke Publishers © 2015 *Reading Power, Revised and Expanded* by Adrienne Gear ISBN 978-1-55138-310-1

Reading Power Home Reading Sheet: Visualize

"Good readers VISUALIZE while they read!"

Name: _____   Date: _____

Title: _____

Author: _____

What I visualized:	What _____ visualized:

I visualized: _____   _____ visualized:

_____   _____

_____   _____

Reading Power Home Reading Sheet: Question

"Good readers ask QUESTIONS while they read!"

Name: _____ Date: _____

Title: _____

Author: _____

While I was reading, I was wondering…

_____ ?

_____ ?

_____ ?

_____ ?

My _____ was wondering…

_____ ?

_____ ?

_____ ?

_____ ?

Pembroke Publishers © 2015 *Reading Power, Revised and Expanded* by Adrienne Gear ISBN 978-1-55138-310-1

Reading Power Home Reading Sheet: Infer

"Good readers INFER while they read!"

Name: _____   Date: _____

Title: _____

Author: _____

In the story:

_____

But I wondered

_____ ?

My _____ wondered

_____ ?

I'm inferring that maybe

_____

My _____'s inferring that maybe

_____

Pembroke Publishers © 2015 *Reading Power, Revised and Expanded* by Adrienne Gear ISBN 978-1-55138-310-1

Reading Power Home Reading Sheet: Transform

"Good readers TRANSFORM their thinking when they read!"

Name: _____ Date: _____

Title: _____

Author: _____

I already knew that _____

_____

My _____ already knew that_____

_____

But after reading this book, I'm now thinking

_____

My _____ is now thinking

_____

Reading Power Questionnaire

Name: _____   Date: _____

Grade: _____

1. What parts of the body do you use when you read?

_____

_____

2. What things did you need to learn in order for you to be able to read?
(E.g., "I need to know the alphabet")

_____

_____

Circle the best answer for you:

1.   When I read, I make connections between what I am reading and my own experiences, other
     books, and the world around me.

       Always   Often   Sometimes   Never

2.   While I'm reading, I ask myself questions about the story.

       Always   Often   Sometimes   Never

3.   While I'm reading, I make pictures in my head about what is happening in the story.

       Always   Often   Sometimes   Never

4.   While I'm reading, I fill in words or pictures in my head that the author didn't include.

       Always   Often   Sometimes   Never

5.   While I'm reading, my ideas, thoughts, and opinions about what I'm reading will change.

       Always   Often   Sometimes   Never

Pembroke Publishers © 2015 *Reading Power, Revised and Expanded* by Adrienne Gear ISBN 978-1-55138-310-1

Reading Power Checklist

Name: _____

Date: _____

Student Name	Connect		Question		Visualize		Infer		Transform	

Pembroke Publishers © 2015 *Reading Power, Revised and Expanded* by Adrienne Gear ISBN 978-1-55138-310-1

Comprehension Assessment

Student Name: _____   Grade: _____   Div: _____

Title: _____

Reading Power	Question	Student Response
Connect	Can you tell me what connecting is? Can you tell me some different ways you can make a connection (to a memory, experience, character, feeling, etc.)? Give me an example of a connection you made to this story.	
Visualize	Can you tell me what visualizing is? Can you tell me about a part in this story where you visualized? What words helped you? Tell me about some other senses you used besides what you saw.	
Question	Can you tell me the difference between a quick question and a deep-thinking question? Give me an example of each from this story and then try to answer them.	
Infer	Can you tell me what inferring is? What are you doing when you infer? What things help you to infer? Give me an example of inferring from this story. Give me a "maybe" thought that you had on this page.	
Transform	Can you tell me what transforming is? When does thinking change when you are reading? Give me an example of how your thinking changed when you read this story.	

Pembroke Publishers © 2015 *Reading Power, Revised and Expanded* by Adrienne Gear ISBN 978-1-55138-310-1

Reading Power Rubric

	Not Meeting	Meeting (Minimal)	Meeting (Fully)	Exceeding
CONNECT	• I cannot draw, write, or make a connection to the story.	• I can talk about what the story reminds me of but can't really explain how it relates to the story. • My connections are *quick* and often don't connect to the meaning of the story. • I might need some prompting by my teacher.	• I can make, write, or draw a connection to the story based on something that has happened to me or something I already know about. • My connections include details that relate to the meaning of the story.	• I can make, write, or draw a connection from my own experience and background knowledge that is related to the meaning of the story. • I can explain how my connection helps me understand the story better. • I consistently and independently make effective connections when I'm reading.
VISUALIZE	• I cannot make mental pictures in my mind when I'm listening to or reading a story.	• I am able to make and draw general mental pictures in my mind, but sometimes these are not connected to the story. • I sometimes need help from my teacher.	• I am able to make and draw visual images that I see in my mind when I read. • My visual images are connected to the story and have some details. • I am able to identify key words from the story that helped me make the mental picture.	• I am able to make, draw, and write about the visual images I see when I read. • I can identify key words and phrases from the story that helped me to visualize. • I can explain how my visual images help me understand the story.
QUESTION	• I am not able to write or ask a question about the story. • It is hard for me to generate a question using a question word.	• I can ask some questions about the story. • Sometimes my questions are not really connected to the meaning of the story. • Sometimes I get mixed up between questions and answers.	• I can ask questions about the story I am reading. • Most of my questions are connected to important parts of the story. • I ask both *quick* and *deep-thinking* questions.	• I can ask questions about the story I am reading or listening to. • My questions are consistently connected to the important parts of the story. • I know the difference between *quick* and *deep-thinking* questions. • I can explain how my questions help me understand the story better.

Pembroke Publishers © 2015 *Reading Power, Revised and Expanded* by Adrienne Gear ISBN 978-1-55138-310-1

Reading Power Rubric (continued)

INFER	• I can tell only the things about the story that I can see in pictures or read in words.	• With help, I can tell one thing about the story that is not written in the text or shown in the pictures. • My inference might not be connected to an important part of the story. • I sometimes need help from my teacher.	• I can tell two things that are not written or shown in the story. • My inferences are important to the meaning of the story. • I can give some reasons for them.	• I can tell three or more things that are not written in the story or shown in the pictures that are important to the meaning of story. • I can give reasons for them, using evidence from the story and my own thinking. • I can explain how my inferences help me understand the story better.
TRANSFORM	• It is difficult for me to summarize the main ideas from story. • I cannot describe any changes in my thinking.	• I can retell most of the main parts of the story. • I can talk about my thinking in relation to the story. • I sometimes need help from my teacher.	• I can summarize the main ideas of the story. • I am able to describe my thinking in some detail in relation to the story I am reading. • I can explain how my thinking has changed using a before-and-after thinking prompt.	• I can summarize the main ideas of the story clearly. • I am aware that stories can sometimes change our thinking. • I can clearly talk and write about how my thinking has changed. • I can explain how my new thinking has helped me understand the story better.

Pembroke Publishers © 2015 *Reading Power, Revised and Expanded* by Adrienne Gear ISBN 978-1-55138-310-1

Final Thoughts

Since its early stages more than ten years ago, I have known in my heart that there was something about Reading Power that made it unique, something about it that was different from other teaching methods or approaches I had tried. First and foremost, it has helped to fill in for me the missing piece of reading instruction—the "thinking" piece. In order for us to help our students become better readers, we need to teach them how to become better thinkers. I believe the power of Reading Power is that it teaches students not what to think, but how to think; it is no longer about filling their minds with facts.

If our goal is teaching students to learn how to think, then we, as their teachers, need to make a strong commitment to achieving that goal:

- considering ourselves teachers of reading no matter what grade we teach
- integrating metacognition into all aspects of our practice
- increasing our instructional time teaching comprehension strategies
- building a common language of reading and thinking across the grades and integrating the language of thinking intentionally into our classrooms, so that students can build on their knowledge of reading and thinking as they progress through their school years
- modeling and demonstrating our thinking voices to students, so that they see what thinking looks like and sounds like
- fostering a transfer of learning by moving from teaching comprehension strategies in isolation to modeling how readers draw from a repertoire of strategies during independent reading
- filling classrooms with rich, thought-provoking literature, and being passionate about the books we share with our students
- helping students believe that they have the "power" to become proficient, interactive readers

---

What else makes Reading Power unique? Madeline Silva, an extraordinary teacher, said to me once that the reason she loved teaching Reading Power so much was that it was "respectful of children's thoughts." Reading Power respects children's thinking by teaching them that their thoughts, their connections, their images, their questions, and their insights are the most important things when it comes to constructing meaning. Reading Power levels the playing field and allows all students, even those who may be burdened by text, a way in.

Heads-Up Teaching

I have been teaching for more than 20 years and, while I recognize that I have grade-level content that I need to teach my students and key concepts I am responsible for covering, these skills and subjects are useless if my students don't understand what I am teaching. More important to me is that after 10 months in my classroom, I have taught my students how to construct meaning; how make sense of the content; how to find those connections, ask the deep questions, and be transformed. I no longer go through the school year with my head down in the curriculum, checking off the boxes as I go. I am a proud to say I now teach with my head up. I look up because I want to see the students I have in front of me—I want to know who they are and hear their voices thinking and wondering and constructing meaning. This is what matters. When dates, names, cities, mathematical equations, and scientific methods have long drifted out of their heads, this is what they will carry with them into the world. Donalyn Miller, author of *The Book Whisperer* said it best: "Instead of standing on a stage each day, dispensing knowledge to my young charges, I should guide them as they approach their own understandings." Reading Power is my way of guiding my students to their own understandings, and that, above all, is what teaching is for.

I also believe that Reading Power has allowed me, and hopefully others, to share the very best books with my students: books that invite us to laugh, sigh, gasp, clap, cry, feel; books that take our breath away and invite us to find pieces of ourselves inside the pages. They are the gifts we get to open every day in our classrooms. Being excited about books in front of your students every day will have far greater impact on their reading development than a boxed reading program that comes in a glossy package with a "bonus book if you order now." And at the end of 10 months in my classroom, what is more important to me than if my students know how to count by 4s, or can tell me the difference between longitude and latitude, is that my students love reading. I want them to join me when I do the "new book" dance on Monday morning as I open up my book bag. I want them to see my tears when I read *Edward Tulane* or hear my laughter when I read *The Book With No Pictures*. I want to see them racing to the shelf to hug the book I just shared. Above all, I want to hear them speak those four words that make my heart smile: "Can we read now?"

Dame Marie Clay, when speaking of her Reading Recovery program for struggling readers, stated, "Making a difference means making it different." I see a parallel here to Reading Power. If we want to make a difference in our students' ability to read and understand, we need to make our teaching different. By teaching students that reading is not just words on a page, but what of ourselves and of our thinking we can bring to those words, by providing them with a common language to use to think and talk about reading, and by sharing extraordinary books with which to read and think about, then I believe we truly can "make a difference." To read is to think—to think is to become. Nothing we teach our children in school could be more powerful.

Professional Resources

Albom, Mitch (2003) *The Five People You Meet in Heaven.* New York, NY: Hyperion.

Allington, Richard. *What Really Matters for Struggling Readers: Designing Research-Based Programs.* Old Tappan, NJ: Pearson.

Anderson, R.C. & Pearson, P. David (1984) "A Schema-Theoretic View of Basic Process in Reading." In *Handbook of Reading Research*, P.D. Pearson (ed.). White Plains, NY: Longman.

Beers, Kylene & Probst, Robert E. (2012) *Notice and Note: Strategies for Close Reading.* Portsmouth, NH: Heinemann.

Beers, Kylene (2002) *When Kids Can't Read—What Teachers Can Do: A Guide for Teachers 6-12.* Portsmouth, NH: Heinemann.

Brownlie, Faye (2005) *Grand Conversations, Thoughtful Responses: A Unique Approach to Literature Circles.* Winnipeg, MN: Portage and Main Press.

Boushey, Gail & Moser, Joan (2006) *The Daily 5: Fostering Literacy Independence in the Elementary Years.* Portland, ME: Stenhouse.

Charlton, James (1991) *The Writer's Quotation Book: A Literary Companion.* New York, NY: Viking.

Dillard, Annie (1989) *The Writing Life.* New York, NY: HarperCollins.

Duffy, Gerald G. & Israel, Susan E (eds) (2008) *Handbook of Research on Reading Comprehension.* London, UK: Routledge.

Fielding, Linda & Pearson, P. David (1994) "Reading Comprehension: What Works?" *Educational Leadership 51*, 5: 62–67.

Gilbar, Steve (1990) *The Readers Quotation Book.* New York, NY: Viking.

Graves, Donald (1991) *Building a Literate Classroom.* New York, NY: Irwin.

Fitzmaurice, Sue (2014) *Angels in the Architecture.* CreateSpace Independent Publishing Platform.

Hall, Susan (1990) *Using Picture Storybooks to Teach Literary Devices.* Phoenix, AZ: Oryx Press.

Harwayne, Shelley (1992) *Lasting Impressions: Weaving Literature into the Writing Workshop.* Portsmouth, NH: Heinemann.

Harvey, Stephanie (1998) *Nonfiction Matters: Reading, Writing, and Research in Grades 3–8.* Portland, ME: Stenhouse.

Harvey, Stephanie & Goudvis, Anne (2000) *Strategies That Work: Teaching Comprehension to Enhance Understanding.* Portland, ME: Stenhouse.

Johnson, Pat & Keier, Katie (2010) *Catching Readers Before They Fall.* Portland, ME: Stenhouse.

Johnston, Peter H. (2004) *Choice Words: How Our Language Affects Children's Learning.* Portland, ME: Stenhouse.

Kamil, Michael L., Pearson, P. David, et al. (2010) *Handbook of Reading Research, Volume IV.* London, UK: Routledge.

Lamont, Anne (1994) *Bird by Bird: Some Instructions on Writing and Life.* New York, NY: Anchor Books.

McCourt, Frank (2005) *Teacher Man.* New York, NY: Charles Scribner.

McGregor, Tanny (2007). *Comprehension Connections: Bridges to Strategic Reading.* Portsmouth, NH: Heinemann.

Michaels, Anne (1996) *Fugitive Pieces.* Toronto, ON: McClelland & Stewart.

Miller, Debbie (2002) *Reading with Meaning: Teaching comprehension in the primary grades.* Portland, ME: Stenhouse.

Miller, Donayln (2009) *The Book Whisperer.* San Francisco, CA: Jossey-Bass.

Morrison, Toni (2006) "The Reader as Artist" *Oprah Magazine*, Volume 7, Number 7.

Pennac, Daniel. *Better Than Life.* (1999) Markham, ON: Pembroke Publishers.

Proulx, Annie (1993) *The Shipping News.* New York, NY: Charles Scribner.

Quindlen, Anna (1998) *How Reading Changed My Life.* New York, NY: Ballantine Books.

Ritchhart, Ron (2011) *Making Thinking Visible: How to Promote Engagement, Understanding and Independence for All Learners.* San Francisco, CA: Jossey-Bass.

Routman, Regie (2014) *Read, Write, Lead.* Alexandria, VA: ASCD.

Routman, Regie (2003) *Reading Essentials: The Specifics You Need to Teach Reading Well.* Portsmouth, NH: Heinemann.

Serravallo, Jennifer (2015) *The Reading Strategies Book: Your Everything Guide to Developing Skilled Readers.* Portsmouth, NH: Heinemann.

Samuels, S. Jay & Farstrup, Alan E. (eds) (2011) *What Research Has to Say About Reading Instruction.* Newark, DE: International Reading Association.

Tovani, Cris (2000) *I Read It, But I Don't Get It.* Portland, ME: Stenhouse.

Thomson, Terry (2015) *The Construction Zone: Building Scaffolds for Readers and Writers.* Portland, ME: Stenhouse.

Wilhelm, Jeff (2010) *Fresh Takes on Teaching Literary Elements: How to Teach What Really Matters About Character, Setting, Points of View and Theme.* New York, NY: Scholastic

Wilkinson, Mary Ruth K. (2000) *A Time to Read: Good Books for Growing Readers.* Vancouver, BC: Regent College Publishing.

Zimmerman, Susan & Keene, Ellin Oliver (1997) *Mosaic of Thought.* Portsmouth, NH: Heinemann.

Index

activity, 13
analyzing, 10
anchor charts
    connecting, 48
    inferring, 112
    questioning, 93–94
    reading power, 151
    transforming, 133
    visualizing, 71
application
    assessment, 172–173
    described, 39, 40
    literature circles, 154–157
    parental involvement, 170–172
    students' use of reading powers, 150–151
assessing goals, 172–173
assessment
    alternatives, 172
    application and, 150–184
    comprehension, 173
    connecting, 54
    described, 172–173
    formal, 173
    goals, 172–173
    inferring, 118
    informal, 173
    literature circles, 157
    questioning, 99
    reading, 22
    traditional, 172
    transformed thinking, 139–140
    visualizing, 77
    whole-class, 173
assign-and-assess teaching, 14, 90

balanced literacy instruction, 16–17
Before, During, and After, 102
BIBB (Bring It Back to the Book)
    strategy, 45, 51, 94
book bins, 33
book collections (books)

alternatives, 37
    book of the month, 171–172
    connecting, 34, 36, 49, 55–57
    creating a collection, 35–37
    inferring, 35, 36
    list, 34–35
    literature circles, 157, 168–170
    one word activity, 135–136
    questioning, 35, 36, 97, 99–100
    reading power, 32–37, 171–172
    rereading, 34
    sources, 36–37
    strategies, 36
    tips, 36
    transforming, 35, 36, 140–142
    visualizing, 34, 36, 77–79
Brain Pockets, 45, 47, 48, 93
    template, 63

Character Venn, 156, 161
Characters I Will Meet, 156, 160
comic books, 110, 115
comprehension
    components of instruction, 39
    defined, 174
    goals, 172–173
    monitoring, 10
    reading, 10, 11, 14, 18, 89, 172–173
    teaching, 17
Comprehension Assessment, 173, 182
comprehension research, 9–11
Connect Books
    finding your, 49, 52
    sample, 53
    strategies, 36
connecting / connections
    anchor chart, 48
    assessing, 54
    booklist, 34, 55–57
    brain pockets, 45

codes, 53
deep-thinking, 50
described, 44
encouraging, 44–45
expanding, 50
extended lessons, 53
going deeper with, 45, 50, 51
group, 49
introducing the power, 46–48
new thinking about, 45
older students, 54
power, 43–66
quick, 50
readers, 44
sequential lessons, 46–54
strategies, 36
song, 43
trading, 51–52
visualizing and, 22
writing extensions, 54
Connecting Stories, 60
Connecting to Me!, 64
constructing meaning, 11, 44
critical thinking, 40, 129–130

decoding, 11, 12, 14, 172, 174
deep-thinking connections, 50
deep-thinking questions, 91–95
    words, 93
determining importance, 10
dialogue creation, 114
drawing inferences, 9
during reading strategies, 15

Evaluating Questions, 96–97, 105
expanding connections, 50
    through writing, 52
Expanding Your Connections, 58–59
extended lessons
    connecting, 53
    questioning, 97–98

visualizing, 76

formal assessment, 173
Four-Corner Visualizing, 80

gems (books for modeling), 36
Gradual Release of Responsibility
  Model, 39
graphic novels, 110
group connect, 49
group participation, 111–112
group practice
  expanding connections, 50
  going deeper with connections,
    51
  group connect, 49
  inferring from very little text, 113
  visualizing on paper together, 72
group questioning, 94
guided practice
  asking and answering questions,
    95
  described, 39, 40, 41
  draw and reflect, 75
  expanding connections, 50
  going deeper with connections,
    51
  group connect, 49
  how reading can change your
    thinking, 138
  inferring from clues, 114
  introducing using your senses, 74
  looking for common themes, 139
  visualizing a character, 75
  visualizing on paper together, 72
  your turn to question, 95–96

home reading, 171

I Wonder…, 101
I'm Okay!, 65
If… Web, 106
illustrations, 115–116
important messages, 136
Independent Connections, 66
independent practice
  asking and answering questions,
    95
  choose your own question book,
    97
  creating a dialogue, 114

described, 39, 40, 41
draw and reflect, 75
expanding connections through
  writing, 52
finding your own connect book,
  52
how reading can change your
  thinking, 138
independent visualizing, 76
inferring from text, 117
inferring with comics, 115
showing how books change your
  thinking, 139
single-image visualizing, 73–74
3, 2, 1 – OWI!, 116–117
trading connections, 51–52
using your senses to visualize, 74
visualizing a character, 75
visualizing on paper on your own,
  73
Independent Visualizing, 86
inferential questions, 90, 96
inferring
  anchor chart, 112
  assessment, 118
  booklist, 35, 118–119
  comic books, 110
  described, 9, 108–110
  games, 111–112
  modeling, 112
  new thinking, 111
  older students, 118
  power, 108–127
  predicting versus, 111
  questioning and, 6, 91, 108
  readers, 109
  reflective journal, 117
  sequential lessons, 111–118
  song, 108
  strategies, 36
  teaching, 109–110
  text, 117
  wordless picture books, 110,
    112–113
Inferring Dialogue, 123
Inferring from Clues, 124
Inferring from Pictures, 120–121
informal assessment, 173
integrated reading / understanding,
  21–22
interacting with text, 19–20

interactive reading / understanding,
  21–22

The Language of Transform, 143
Letter to the Author, 165–166
life experiences, 44
Listening for Picture Words, 87
Lit Circle Assessment Rubric, 158
Lit Circle Discussion Record, 158
literal questions, 90, 96
literal reading / understanding,
  21–22
literature circles
  additional response activities,
    156–157
  assessment, 157
  before starting, 155
  benefits of, 154
  recommended books, 157,
    168–170
  recommended year plan, 154
  reading powers and, 154–157
  sample set-up, 155
  starting, 156
Little _____ _____, 107
Looking for What Matters Most, 149

Making a Difference, 146
making connections
  described, 9, 45
  experience and, 25
  quiet, 39, 48
  rubric, 54
Making Connections template,
  61–62
metacognition/metacognitive
  defined, 9, 18, 151, 174
  described, 17–19
  enhancing, 19
  helping students become, 27
  reinforcing, 92
  self-monitoring versus, 151
  thinking prompts, 41
method of instruction, 22
modeling
  reading power instruction, 37–40
  teacher, 37, 39–40
moral ethic, 129–130
morning reading, 171

New Words, 167

Noticing How My Thinking Changes, 147
novel studies, 154

older students
    connecting, 54
    inferring, 118
    questioning, 98
    transforming, 139
    visualizing, 76
One Word Activity, 144–145
OWI, 115–117
    template, 125
OWI with Text, 127

parent night, 171
parent information bookmark, 171
parents
    book of the month, 171–172
    home reading, 171
    morning reading, 171
    parent night, 171
    reading power and, 170–172
    school newsletters, 171
    strategy of the month, 171
phonemic awareness, 12, 24
Photo Album, 163
picture books
    book collections, 33
    Connect Book, 52
    inferring with, 112
    wordless, 110, 112–113
picture words, 69
poetry, 76
post-reading strategies, 15
predicting, 111
pre-reading strategies, 15
proficient readers, 27, 91, 155
    profile, 9–10, 12

questioning
    anchor chart, 93–94
    assessment, 99
    booklist, 35, 36, 97, 99–100
    described, 90
    extended lessons, 97–98
    group, 94
    inferring and, 6, 91, 108
    new thinking, 91–92
    older students, 98
    power, 89–107

readers, 91
sequential lessons, 92–98
song, 89
strategies, 36
teaching, 90
words, 91–92, 93
questions
    answering, 89–90
    asking, 9, 91, 92
    deep-thinking, 91–95
    important (that matter), 91
    inferential, 90
    literal, 90
    quick, 91–92, 93, 95
Quick and Deep-Thinking Questions, 103
quick connections, 50
"quiet connections thumbs-up" system, 39, 48
quick questions, 91–92, 93, 95

read-aloud (reading aloud), 33, 38, 39, 170
reading
    current practice, 15–16
    home, 171
    instruction components, 39, 40–41
    integrated, 22
    interactive, 22
    levels, 21–22
    literal, 22
    morning, 171
    teaching, 11, 13–14
    thinking, 13–14, 27, 137, 138
    three-dimensional (3D), 130
    three stages of teaching, 15–16
    two-dimensional (2D), 130
reading assessment, 22
reading comprehension
    assessments of, 172
    common language of, 18
    described, 10, 11
    goals, 172–173
    subjectivity of, 14
    traditional, 89
Reading Power(s)
    anchor chart, 151
    book collections, 32–37
    book of the month, 171–172

components of instruction, 39, 40–41
connecting, 43–66
described, 13, 174
guide for parents, 174
inferring, 108–127
instruction, 37–41
key concepts, 17–22
literature circles, 154–157
myths, 23–26
notebooks, 52
origins of, 11–12
parents, 170–172
program components, 22, 27–42
promoting use of, 150–151
questioning, 89–107
students using, 150–151
teaching, 22, 24–25
theme song, 32
time for, 17
transforming, 128–149
using, 22–23
visualizing, 67–88
Reading Power Checklist, 181
Reading Power Guide for Parents, 174
Reading Power Home Reading Sheets
    Connect, 175
    Infer, 178
    Question, 177
    Transform, 179
    Visualize, 176
Reading Power Questionnaire, 180
Reading Power Rubric, 183–184
Reading Powers Model, 27–31
Reading Program, 16–17
reading skills, 11
Reading Voice/Thinking Voice, 148
reflective journal
    connecting, 53
    inferring, 117
    questioning, 97
    transforming, 139
    visualizing, 76
respecting children's thoughts, 185
rubrics
    connecting, 54
    inferring, 118
    literature circle, 158
    questioning, 99

reading power, 183–184
transformed thinking, 140
visualizing, 77

schema, 46
school newsletters, 171
self-monitoring, 151
Setting Map, 162
Single-Image Visualizing, 82
"something happening", 14
song lyrics, 151
speaking voice, 38
strategy of the month, 171
Story Scenes, 81
strategy, 13
student participation
    one word activity, 134–136
    thinking changes as we read,
      137
summarizing, 130
synthesis, 21, 131
synthesizing, 10, 130–132

Talking Balloons and Thinking
  Bubbles, 122
Talking Bubble, 38, 42, 122
teacher directed / guided
    asking questions that matter,
      94–95
    a change in thinking, 134
    exploring deep-thinking ques-
      tions, 93
    finding the important message,
      136
    group questioning, 94
    inferring from illustrations,
      115–116
    inferring from very little text, 113
    inferring from wordless books,
      112–113
    introducing inferring through
      games, 111–112
    introducing the power of trans-
      forming, 132–133
    introducing the power to connect,
      46–48
    introducing the power to ques-
      tion, 92
    introducing the power to visual-
      ize, 69–71

    looking for what matters most,
      137–138
    modeling visualizing on paper, 72
    modeling your thinking, 48
    one word activity, 134–136
    OWI with text, 117
    quick and deep-thinking, 50
    thinking changes as we read, 137
teacher modeling, 37, 39–40
teaching
    assign-and-assess, 14
    comprehension, 17
    direct, 37
    explicit, 40
    heads-up, 186
    reading powers, 22
    reading, thinking and, 13–14
    thinking, 185
themes, 139
think-alouds (thinking aloud), 25,
  38, 39, 170
thinking
    articulating, 18
    awareness of, 18, 92, 172
    books and, 139
    changes in, 134
    common language, 21
    critical, 40, 129–130
    higher-level, 109
    modeling, 48
    reading, 13–14, 27, 137, 138
    strategic, 170
    teaching, 13–14, 27, 185
    thinking about your, 18
    transformed, 134
    what it looks like, 29, 31
thinking brain, 29–31
Thinking Bubble, 38, 42, 122
thinking voice, 38
three stages of teaching reading,
  15–16
3, 2, 1 – OWI!, 126
transforming / transformation
    anchor chart, 133
    assessment, 139–140
    booklist, 35, 140–142
    chant, 128
    defined, 129
    described, 129–132
    older students, 139

    power, 128–149
    readers, 130
    reflective journal, 139
    sequential lessons, 132–139
    song, 128
    strategies, 36, 131
    summarizing, 130
    synthesizing, 130–132
    teaching, 131
Transforming My Thinking, 164

understanding text, 21–22
Using My Reading Powers, 153
Using our Senses, 83

Visualize, Draw, and Reflect, 84–85
visualizing
    activity, 70–71
    anchor chart, 71
    assessing, 77
    booklist, 34, 77–79
    chant, 67
    characters, 75
    connecting and, 22
    described, 9, 67–68
    exercises, 69
    extended lesson, 76
    independent, 76
    new thinking, 68
    older students, 76
    on paper, 72–73
    power, 67–88
    readers, 68
    sequential lessons, 69–76
    senses, 74
    single-image, 73–74
    song, 67
    strategies, 36
Visualizing Poetry, 88
vocabulary, 11, 68, 157

Weekly Thinking Page, 159
What Are You Wondering?, 104
What? So What?, 152
wordless picture books, 110,
  112–113
writing
    expanding connections through,
      52
    extensions, 54